The Business Owner's

ESSENTIAL GUIDE

TO **I.T.** & ALL THINGS **DIGITAL**

Information Technology

Published by CelebrityPress®, Orlando, FL

CelebrityPress® is a registered trademark.

Printed in the United States of America.

ISBN: 978-0-9912143-2-7
LCCN: 2014900536

This publication is designed to provide accurate and authoritative information with regard to the subject matter covered. It is sold with the understanding that the publisher is not engaged in rendering legal, accounting, or other professional advice. If legal advice or other expert assistance is required, the services of a competent professional should be sought. The opinions expressed by the authors in this book are not endorsed by Celebrity Press® and are the sole responsibility of the author rendering the opinion.

Most CelebrityPress® titles are available at special quantity discounts for bulk purchases for sales promotions, premiums, fundraising, and educational use. Special versions or book excerpts can also be created to fit specific needs.

For more information, please write:
CelebrityPress®
520 N. Orlando Ave, #2
Winter Park, FL 32789
or call 1.877.261.4930

Visit us online at: www.CelebrityPressPublishing.com

The Business Owner's

ESSENTIAL GUIDE

TO **I.T.** & ALL THINGS **DIGITAL**

Information Technology

CELEBRITY PRESS®
Winter Park, Florida

CONTENTS

CHAPTER 1

CUSTOMER SERVICE

BY DAVID AND CATHY SZYMANSKI

As business owners of a professional technology provider firm, we believe very strongly in the importance of "wowing" our customers by extending to them customer service that far exceeds their expectations. We are committed to keeping our customers happy by providing them with the same service we would expect if we were the customer. That's also how we want our employees to treat our customers.

In general, professional technology providers will offer similar types of equipment, monitoring services and support. Granted, there may be some providers that have more knowledge, skill and expertise, but for the most part, the offerings are going to be very similar. The big distinguishing factor between providers will be their level of customer service.

When we talk to our customers we treat them as though they were the only person in the world. We aren't checking our text messages, emails or voicemails during the conversation. We are eye to eye with them and they have our full attention. Being able to empathize with the customer is extremely important and giving them our undivided attention plays a big role in conveying to them our genuine concern.

If the customer sees their problem as a huge problem, then we need to respond to it as a huge problem. It doesn't matter what we think, it's all about what the customer thinks. It is vitally important for us to fully understand the customer's point of view. They are looking at the problem from the perspective of their livelihood and if the problem isn't fixed quickly, it will interfere with their ability to make money and pay their employees. From the customer's perspective, if they can't provide excellent customer service to their customers because of a technology issue, then they run the risk of losing business. We need to see it the same way and have the same sense of urgency. Our customers need assurance from us that everything will be OK.

DEVELOPING A CUSTOMER SERVICE CULTURE

Our employees are more than just employees to us. They are highly-valued team members. We all work together to accomplish the common goal of superior service and undeniable customer satisfaction. To this end, we provide each of our team members four weeks of training per year at conferences or various industry-related training sessions. We do everything possible to enable our technicians to stay up to date on the most recent advancements in the industry so they are prepared to deliver world-class service to our customers. Also, if there is a new process that will be implemented for a customer, we have systems set up in our office to test the application on our own machines to make sure the installation for our customer will be flawless.

Each of our employees have the autonomous authority to do whatever is necessary to fix the problem for the customer so we don't have to go through an escalation process to get the issue resolved. We had an incident recently where one of our customers had a slight emergency and needed a technician at their facility as soon as possible. Because we were two hours away, one of our team members made the decision to hire a technician in the same city as our customer to take care of the problem. The hired technician was able to get there within minutes, whereas it would have taken our technician more than two hours to arrive at the location. Our team member didn't have to ask for permission because he knew he had the authority to do whatever was in the best interest of our customer.

Customer service should not be a department in a company, it should be a culture that permeates every department and is exemplified by every employee. Often when companies have someone contact them with a problem, they refer them to customer service or the resolution department. In our company, everyone is the customer service department. We don't pass the problem off to anyone else.

In Jim Collins book *Good to Great,* he talks about what separates the great companies from the merely good ones over the long term. One of the things that he found from his research was that great companies have a greater purpose and bigger vision beyond just making money or being number one. A lot of companies fall into the trap of just focusing on making money, and then they never become a great company.

One of our team members recently was driving in the vicinity of one of our customers and thought, "I haven't talked to that customer in a while." So he made a quick stop at a nearby bakery, bought some delicious cookies, and delivered them to their office simply as a kind gesture because he hadn't seen them in a while. Interestingly, even though it was intended to be just a friendly visit, he walked away with a sale to that customer. You see, this culture of customer service is always on the minds of our team members. In fact, customer service is contagious in our office. When great customer service is exemplified, it is celebrated within our team and it becomes viral.

Even when a potential employee is interviewing with us, at each stage of our four-step interview process we emphasize the importance of customer service in our work. We also ask our team members to observe what people are doing in other service industries in relationship to customer service. If they are in a mall and see a great example of customer service, we ask them to think about how that may translate into our business.

CUSTOMERS MUST FEEL VALUED

We do everything possible to make sure our customers know we value them and their time. In fact, we pay our customers $1.00 for every minute we are late for an appointment. If we say we will be there by 1 p.m., but our tech doesn't arrive until 1:15 p.m., we will credit them $15.00. We strongly believe that our customers' time is just as valuable, or more valuable, as that of our team members. Be assured, very seldom are we late for an appointment.

If we ever make a mistake, we never make up stories to cover up our error. If a customer calls to tell us one of our team members was supposed to be at their office at 9 a.m. and that team member isn't there because he simply forgot (which very rarely happens), we will tell the customer he forgot. We won't tell them he's stuck in traffic or had an emergency call he needed to make. We will be straightforward and honest with each of our customers. In customer service and in every aspect of life, honesty is truly the best policy. Our honest approach with our customers has enabled us to build relationships based on trust.

We can't guarantee that we won't make mistakes, but if we do make a mistake, we guarantee we will be honest about it and get it corrected promptly. We try to turn lemons into lemonade by putting the customer in a better position. For example, we had a customer whose computers were running slow for about 20 hours while we were doing some maintenance on them. To compensate, we bought a $700 add on to make their computers faster. By doing something like installing an upgraded application or giving them a monetary credit, they realize we are committed to them, respect their time and their technology needs. Stepping up to take ownership of a mistake, showing respect, and giving some form of compensation goes a long way to smooth out any relationship wrinkles that may have occurred as a result of our error.

After every service call by one of our team members, we ask the customer to fill out a survey related to the service they received. As part of the survey, we always give the customer the opportunity to tell us how we can improve our service. Our team members genuinely want to know if there is any way they can improve their service to our customers because they are deeply committed to wowing and impressing them. We value their opinions and take their survey responses very seriously.

CUSTOMER SERVICE IS BASED ON RELATIONSHIPS

Several years ago when Microsoft would sponsor launch events for their newest products, we took our team of techs to the event. We had such a good time that we thought we should expand this type of activity to include our customers. So, when an industry event would take place we began renting a bus that we called the "party bus" and invited our customers to attend the event with us. We incorporated snacks, games and educational sessions on the bus ride and customers began looking forward to these events. Then we expanded it to trips to amusement parks or other fun destinations. We then opened the "party bus" up to the immediate families of our staff and customers and took them to these fun destination points. Everyone got to know each other better and our customers would tell others that Szymanski Consulting took them on a trip. We pay for their bus ride, their meals and their admission to the amusement park or destination point. While it is a significant expense to undertake, we really believe it is an investment in our customers and their families and we ultimately benefit from building that relationship with them.

Part of building a strong relationship with a client is understanding their goals. To provide the best customer service we must have an intimate knowledge of what is going on with our customers. It is also helpful to know what our customers are doing with their customers. We need to understand how they do their job. That's how we can help them make technological improvements to their process. In order to differentiate ourselves we need to help our customers improve their processes and become more efficient. Unless you know how your customer's employees are working, you will not be able to assist them in increasing their efficiency and productivity.

When we meet with our customers or prospective customers we share with them our goals and they share with us their goals and growth plans. Together, we determine how we can best help them in their future plans. We can assist our customers with their plans as well as the IT portion of their budget. For a lot of our customers we are their IT department.

When our customers are constructing a new building or doing expansion remodeling, we work closely with the architect, contractors and our customer's staff to determine the most efficient logistical layout for their technology needs. We will be there from the beginning design work through the final installation. We have had situations where a company moves their physical location from one building to another. When the employees leave on Friday we begin moving all their technology equipment to the new location. As a result of our behind the scenes work, when they come in Monday morning to the new building they are able to go to work as though they have always worked in that new building.

Our team members walk the halls and interact with employees when they are onsite at a customer's location. Every week our team members will have conversations with technology users in their office to help us discover any issues that may exist or any areas that can be improved. In one instance, one of our team member noticed people dropping off

USB drives with files on them. When we discovered this was happening we recommended to the customer that they begin utilizing a file transfer service as a much more efficient way to share files. The customer didn't even know something like that existed even though that type of service has been around for quite a long time. By our team members simply walking around an office and talking to the staff we are often able to solve problems our customers didn't even know they had. That's part of our goal. If we make our customers more efficient, then we are offering them the kind of customer service they expect and deserve. If we are able to help our customers expand and grow then we will expand and grow with them.

EXAMPLES OF OUTSTANDING CUSTOMER SERVICE

We received a call from the owner of a radio station. He explained to us that when inspecting the remodeling for their grand opening he was extremely disappointed with the inconsistencies in size of the computer monitors and the overall technology arrangement. He asked us if there was anything we could do to resolve his dilemma. He wasn't one of our customers, but he needed our help. We took our team into his studio that evening and revamped it in one night. We pulled the monitors from our office and from our homes to put into his studio so there would be a consistent look to those that would be attending the grand opening event. It looked very impressive and the owner was extremely pleased.

In another incident, the sister of one of our customers was traveling in the Middle East and was unable to connect to the hotel WIFI. This often happens, especially when people travel abroad. The hotel was not able or willing to respond to her request for connection assistance until the next day and we were contacted to intercede in the dilemma. We communicated with her directly via an international call and were able to walk her through several trouble shooting steps until the problem was discovered and the issue was resolved. Unfortunately, the hotel did not have the level of customer service to assist her, but we were able to help her from across the ocean.

In a final example of outstanding customer service, one of our nursing home customers experienced a water main break in the middle of the night and had six inches of water in the section of building where the server room was located. Our team members went to the building at

3:00 a.m. to relocate all of their servers to another part of the building. We were there before any other disaster restoration services arrived on the scene.

MAKE SURE YOUR TECHNOLOGY PROVIDER IS CUSTOMER SERVICE ORIENTED

Customer service is an art, and not every technology provider will deliver the same level of customer service. If you are looking for a company to assist you with your technology needs, make sure customer service is at the top of your "must have" list. Talk to other businesses that have used the technology firm you are considering to find out not only their level of technical expertise, but also their level of customer service and commitment to make sure your business needs are just as important to them as they are to you.

About Cathy

I am very fortunate that I got to fulfill my dream of working in customer service and WOWING clients.

After six years in the Army and Army Reserves, I moved to Erie to attend school, fell in love with Erie, Pennsylvania, and knew it was where I wanted to stay. After graduation, I got a job as the Service Manager at GTE Mobilnet, which is now Verizon Wireless.

My husband David and I met at GTE Mobilnet and married 18 months later. Although I loved my job, helping David at Szymanski Consulting was an offer I just could not refuse. My title is the Director of WOW, and my job is to make sure that each customer experience is a WOW experience. Our philosophy is simple, we treat others as we would like to be treated. This philosophy has allowed our company to grow and prosper with long-term customers. We are not looking for quick sales, we are building long-term relationships.

Szymanski Consulting is a long-standing member of the Manufacturer's Association, Chamber of Commerce, Erie Network Users Group and Technology Council of Northwest Pennsylvania. Ten years ago I started a computer facility management support company, 'E-IT Support' to complement Szymanski Consulting's offerings, and, more recently, have co-authored a book, *Computers Should Just Work.*

In my spare time my passion is volunteering. I love helping children and making our community a better place. I am on the board for Community Shelter Services, secretary for Auto Racers for Kids, and treasurer for Happy Scrappers Quilt Guild. I am the vice president of Pennsylvania State Police Camp Cadet Program, and the Pennsylvania District Chair for Growth for Kiwanis International. I am a past Distinguished Governor for the Pennsylvania District of Kiwanis, where, with my team of 22,000 volunteers, we set records for community service. I can be found volunteering wherever there is a need in the community.

David and I have two Dachshunds and one Maine Coon cat – Wilbur, Oscar and Roxie – and enjoy traveling, gardening, reading and biking.

You can connect with Cathy at cathy@szy.com

CHAPTER 2

WHAT TO LOOK FOR IN AN IT PROVIDER?

BY BILL OOMS

If you've been in business any length of time, it's very possible you have a story or two you have told your friends or business acquaintances about an Information Technology (IT) mishap that has taken place in your company because of an error made by a less than competent technician. There are no shortages of horror stories about incompetent technology personnel who have caused more problems for the company they were supposed to be helping.

As with any industry, the quality of workmanship and professionalism within the IT vertical will range on the spectrum from superior to poor. Unfortunately, the trade even has its share of individuals that act in ways that are deceitful, dishonest, and unethical. Sometimes this undesirable behavior is driven by greed for money, but more often it's simply because they don't have the skills and competency necessary to resolve the issue in the right way. As a result, they will try to cover up their inadequacies by offering misleading or incorrect information accompanied by a poor work ethic, inadequate management skills, and pitiful customer service efforts.

You may or may not know that there is no regulation or established standards within this industry. That fact is a major reason there is such a variation in competence in the technology repair and consulting field. Literally anyone can claim to be an IT professional. In fact, many of the technology businesses today were started because the current owner was fired or laid off from their job and couldn't find work anywhere else. That means many of the so-called "experts" are less than qualified to handle many technology issues faced by the growing demands of today's business world.

Think about it. Automotive mechanics, electricians, plumbers, lawyers, doctors, dentists, realtors, accountants, etc. are all heavily regulated to protect the consumer from receiving substandard work or from being deceived. There is a formal complaint, investigation, and disciplinary process in place in each state if any regulated professional violates the standards to which they have agreed to adhere. Unfortunately, this is not so in the world of technology. There are independent IT certifications that can be obtained, but there are no regulatory standards to which these individuals must adhere.

The good news is, despite the contingent of lackluster technicians as described above, there are a lot of very qualified and ethical technology consultants available today. Don't allow the previous paragraphs to discourage you in your search for an outstanding tech firm with which you can place your confidence and entrust the technology side of your business. They are definitely out there and this chapter will help you find the right fit for your business.

IMPORTANT CONSIDERATIONS WHEN HIRING YOUR IT PROVIDER

Below are numerous critical issues you must consider when hiring your IT provider. These considerations are arranged in the areas of Customer Service, Maintenance and Monitoring of Your Network, Backups and Disaster Recovery, and Technical Expertise and Support. When interviewing a prospective technology provider, make sure your investigation includes these very important matters as they relate to your working relationship. They will prove to be vitally important to the selection of the right technology firm for your business.

CUSTOMER SERVICE

Accessibility
Any reputable consultant will answer their phones live during their normal business hours, which will typically be from 8 a.m. to 5 p.m.

However, there should also be an after-hours emergency number, including weekends, that you can call if a problem arises. We all know that problems don't always occur during normal business hours and you need to be assured your IT provider will be available when needed.

Guaranteed Response Time

It is imperative that your consultant can guarantee in writing to have a technician working on your problem within a certain time frame after you call. This document is called a Service Level Agreement (SLA) and should be standard protocol for your provider.

Listening Skills and Appropriate Responses

Good consulting firms will train their entire staff to excel in customer service. This begins with listening to a client's concerns, understanding them, and responding to them in understandable terms. The technician should have the "heart of a teacher" and be willing to take time to thoroughly answer your questions. When you ask a question you should not be made to feel stupid by the response you receive. If the technician comes across as arrogant or impatient with your questions, that's not the person you want to use as your IT provider.

Proactive Approach

Your provider should routinely and proactively conduct regular technology business review meetings with you to look for new ways to help improve your operations, lower your costs and increase efficiencies. Their goal should be to help your business become more efficient, profitable and competitive in your marketplace. These meetings should at least be annually, but may be as often as monthly, depending on your business needs.

Clear and Detailed Invoicing

Invoicing details from your provider should never be a secret. Each invoice should definitively show the work that has been done, why it was done, when it was done, and how much time was spent on the task.

Properly Insured

If your provider causes a problem with your network that results in loss of hours, days, data or revenue, the provider needs to be held liable. If your provider is not properly insured, the chances of your recovering any monetary damages will be minimized. Additionally, if one of their technicians is injured while at your office, your provider must provide worker's compensation to cover their employee's injury and the resulting lost wages.

A few years ago one of the big box electronic stores were served multiple lawsuits from customers for damages incurred as a result of their technicians' unethical and irresponsible behavior. The technicians were copying and distributing personal information obtained from their customers' personal computers and laptops brought in for repair. One customer's laptop was lost and the employee tried to cover up the negligence. These unfortunate types of activities are evidence you need to make sure your provider is properly insured for your own protection.

Guaranteed Completion Time and Budget

It is imperative to have a fixed price and a guaranteed completion time in writing from your provider. A reputable provider will have no problem giving this to you. Don't allow a provider to quote only "time and materials" because it leaves the door open for additional add-ons that could become very costly.

MAINTENANCE AND MONITORING OF YOUR NETWORK

Remote Monitoring

Your provider should insist on remotely monitoring your network 24-7-365 to keep critical security settings, virus definitions and security patches up to date and to prevent problems from turning into downtime, viruses, lost data or other issues. If your provider will not commit to this type of monitoring, don't do business with them. An effective remote network monitoring system will keep your business secure and will alert your provider to potential problems that can be addressed before they become bigger problems resulting in network downtime.

Monthly Reports

A reputable provider will provide you with a monthly report that shows all the updates, security patches and the status of every machine on your network so you know for sure your systems have been secured and updated. These reports will show you on a regular basis the overall health score of your network and the updates to your antivirus, security settings, patches, hard drive space, backups, speed and performance, etc.

Network Documentation

It should be standard procedure for your provider to supply you with written documentation detailing what software licenses you own, critical passwords, user information, hardware inventory, etc. In essence, these are the "keys to the kingdom." It is imperative that you not allow your IT provider to solely hold this information. If they are the only ones to hold this information they could block you from your own business. While it is highly unlikely this would happen, you must never take that risk. Every business should have this information willingly shared with them by their IT provider in written and electronic form at no additional cost. Your provider should also perform a quarterly update on this material and make sure certain key people from your organization have this information and know how to use it. This enables you to have complete control over your network.

Again, you should never allow an IT person to have sole control over this information. This translates into them having control over you and your entire company. If your provider refuses or is reluctant to share this information with you, do not enter into a working relationship with them.

Capable Staff of Technicians

Your provider should have detailed network documentation and updates on your account enabling any of their technicians to be able to pick up where another one has left off. If your regular technician becomes ill or takes an extended vacation, other technicians should be able to step right in without any disruption to your business workflow. They should be as familiar with your network and processes as your regular technician.

All-Inclusive Managed Service Plan

One of the more popular service plans offered by provider firms today is an "all-inclusive" managed service plan. These plans are good things to have because they will save you a lot of time and money in the long run. However, make sure you really understand what is and isn't included in the plan. Sometimes what is offered as an "all-inclusive" managed support plan isn't always as "all-inclusive" as you might think. You should be fully aware of any possible "gotcha's" hidden in the fine print. The following is a list of things you will want to consider:

Are phone and email helpdesk included?

Are network upgrades, moves, and adding or removing users included?

Are hardware and/or software included?

What about 3rd party software support?

What are the costs/consequences of early cancellation?

What if you aren't happy with their services? Do they offer a money-back guarantee?

If the hardware and software are included, what happens if you cancel the contract?

Is offsite backup included and to what degree?

If you have a major disaster, is restoring your network included?

Are onsite support calls and support to remote offices included?

Are home PCs used to access the company's network after hours included?

Whenever you enter into a contract, you should always have legal counsel review your agreement, especially if it involves a lengthy and expensive project. The money you spend on a qualified attorney will go a long way to ensure a trouble free project.

BACKUPS AND DISASTER RECOVERY

On-Site and Off-Site Backups

Your provider should insist on monitoring an off-site as well as an on-site backup system for your business. There are a variety of backup systems you can utilize and a qualified provider can help you determine what backup system will work best for your situation. Personally, I would never allow any business in today's environment to use tape backups because they are extremely unreliable and there are much safer systems available. Your provider company should be able to give you 24/7 monitoring with backups every 15 minutes, an off-site storage option, data restores as needed, and a virtualized server in case of a disaster.

Testing Your Backup System

You won't know if your backup system works unless you test it. Many businesses that don't use a professional IT provider often miss this very important step in their backup plan. Your provider should regularly perform a test restore from backup to make sure your data can be recovered in the event of an emergency. The worst time to "test" a backup is when you desperately need your data restored.

Back Up Before Upgrading Equipment and Software

A qualified provider will insist on backing up your network BEFORE performing any type of project or upgrade. This is a simple precaution in case a hardware failure or software glitch causes a major problem.

Written Disaster Recovery Plan

Your provider must be able to quickly restore your data and network in case of a disaster and this plan must be in writing. It should also be part of your overall business disaster recovery plan that is made available to the appropriate individuals within your organization.

TECHNICAL EXPERTISE AND SUPPORT

Qualified and Knowledgeable Help Desk

We have all experienced those customer service calls when we are connected to another country and have no choice but to try to understand someone that has such an extreme foreign accent that it makes the conversation painstakingly difficult to understand. You feel exhausted and frustrated at the conclusion of those calls. You don't need that type of anxiety when communicating with your IT provider help desk. Making sure your provider has an in-house help desk, staffed with cooperative, friendly, helpful and easy-to-understand staff is a very important consideration. Make sure they don't outsource this service to a third party or overseas. You don't want someone with no knowledge of your company trying to assist you. This only creates confusion and delays. You want to work with people you know and trust.

Ticketing System

Your provider must have a well-run ticketing system to track issues and resolutions. A good ticketing system will enable your provider to quickly look up any problem they already encountered and the associated fix. This will prevent redundant research time and enable a prompt response to your current issue.

Promptness and Professional Appearance

When technicians work on-site at your location they should arrive on time and they should be dressed professionally. Your provider should be very proud of the promptness and professionalism of their technicians and you should feel comfortable having them in your office.

Qualified to Support Your Unique Line of Business Applications

Your provider must be familiar with and be able to support your unique line of business applications. They should also take ownership of the problems of all your business applications, even if they didn't install it. That doesn't necessarily mean they can fix faulty software, but they should be the liaison between you and your vendor to resolve any problems you are having and make sure these applications work smoothly for you.

Taking Ownership of Your IT Needs

When something goes wrong with your Internet service, phone systems, printers or other IT services, your IT provider should "own" the problem so you don't have to worry about trying to resolve any of these issues. You don't want a provider that will say, "That's not our problem to fix." A provider that is willing to take ownership is a provider that will serve you well.

DEVELOP A LASTING PARTNERSHIP AND RELATIONSHIP WITH YOUR IT PROVIDER

After selecting your provider, it will be in your best interest to develop a long-term relationship with them. They can save you time and money by increasing your efficiencies and giving you a competitive edge. Not every relationship will work out, but when you find a good relationship, stick with it and build on it.

In addition to the great customer service you receive from your IT provider, there may be other business benefits to having a long-term relationship. Your IT provider will interact with possibly hundreds of businesses over the course of time. There may be opportunity for your provider to refer business to you based on the solid relationship you have built. Of course, you may also refer business to your IT provider. This can definitely be a win-win strategy.

About Bill

Bill Ooms has over 30 years of experience in computer consulting. His business and economics education from Purdue, along with his experience, help Bill provide cost-effective recommendations for using today's technology to meet the needs of small businesses. He has consulted for major corporations as well as dozens of small businesses. He has developed several applications, taught classes, worked extensively with networks and the Internet, and has designed and planned various systems. Bill currently is president of the Greater Lafayette Information Technology Society, and is serving on the Board of Directors for the Greater Lafayette Public Transportation Corporation.

As president and owner of Business System Solutions, which is based in West Lafayette, Indiana, Bill has focused on customer service to meet the IT needs for small businesses. Bill's clients consider him an expert at all things technical. His goal is to help business owners gain incredible peace of mind by eliminating costly, frustrating, and time-consuming problems that most businesses have with technology.

Business System Solutions specializes in providing management and support for all technology in small businesses. This includes support for computer networks and working with hardware and software vendors whose technology is used by those businesses. They do this with friendly, proactive, and responsive service.

Bill is the author of *Small Business IT* in which he gives advice on how to find the right computer consultant for your business. He also gained recognition in 2013 for co-authoring the book *The Tech (Multiplier)* which received Amazon Bestseller status in seven different categories.

CHAPTER 3

DATA BACKUP:
IT'S ALL ABOUT RECOVERY

BY CARL SCALZO

Data backup, especially at the enterprise level, is an essential security measure in today's computing environment. The loss of valuable data can cripple a business, if not destroy it entirely. Many companies mistakenly roll the dice on their data by not having any kind of backup system in place, or trying to backup their data in the least expensive way possible. When it comes to data, as with most things in life, cheap is not the best solution nor is it the proper way to determine your backup modality.

The key to data backup is having the end in mind. If you have collected data, but don't know what you want to do with it, having it becomes irrelevant. You can back up a whole host of data and it could take two years to recover, but was anything accomplished? Will you use the recovered data? Again, what will be its end use?

RPO AND RTO CONSIDERATIONS

When creating your backup, it is important to understand your Recovery Point Objectives (RPO) and Recovery Time Objectives (RTO). RPO is referencing the points during your business cycle when you want to have your data backed up. For example, if you designate your backup time to be 5:00 p.m. every day, you are saying that if you have a system failure resulting in the loss of data at 4:30 p.m. today you would be OK not having a backup of all the work done today. If that is not acceptable, more backups will be necessary. Keep in mind, the more often you backup, the higher backup costs will be. As a business owner, you will have to determine backup points based on your specific data capture needs, the cost to backup the data, and the cost of not having a data backup for certain intervals of time.

RTO is the amount of time that lapses from when a disaster strikes to when you get your data restored. What timeframe do you consider acceptable for the retrieval of your data? Will tomorrow be acceptable or can you wait a week? Or, will you need it within hours or minutes?

WHAT ARE YOU BACKING UP?

Another important consideration is what you are backing up. The more you back up, the longer it will take to recover and subsequently the more expensive it will be. It can also potentially be more complicated. For example, if I were to back up your personal laptop, would I need to back up just your document files or would I also need to back up all your pictures and music as well? Apply this same principle to your business. What files and documents are really important? It is necessary to rank the importance of these files as they pertain to the continuation of your business. What files will you need first, second, third, etc.?

When thinking of backup, you need to think in terms of what to backup, how often to do the backup, how long to do the backup, and the order of the backup. What files do you backup first? Do you backup the payroll files first? Or maybe the HR files go first? You have to think of what files are a priority to recover. For example, you may want to backup your financial system 16 times a day. But you may feel comfortable backing up your Word documents just once every day.

I had an interesting situation with a business that had to recover a tremendous amount of data. They had about 15 terabytes of data which is an extremely large amount. Unfortunately, the way they backed up their data took about 10 days to recover. They backed it up just to the cloud and didn't make a local copy. During the restore they were looking for specific files, but those files were at the tail end of the backup, and the backup mechanism they used didn't have the ability to search for specific files. So, they had to restore all 15 terabytes of data and wait for the entire restore to complete before getting to the files they needed most. They were without a substantial amount of their files for almost a month.

To add insult to injury, when they initially made the backup, they didn't backup any of the security privileges so they couldn't even put the data back into their production environment. They had the data, but there was no way to determine who had access to it prior to recovery. In order to put the data back into production, they would have to give all 200 employees access to 100% of the data.

In this scenario, the company looked at backup as just a backup process. They failed to look at it from the recovery perspective. The approach they took was to implement a "cheap" backup. In the end, their "cheap" solution cost them a tremendous amount of down time and a lot more money than they would have spent for a robust backup system.

They have since contracted with my firm to properly backup their data. Now there is a backup to the cloud, a backup locally, and there are multiple copies. If they lose data today they can retrieve it instantly from their onsite server. Or, if their local server is destroyed in a fire, they can retrieve their data from the cloud backup.

NO COOKIE-CUTTER BACKUP SYSTEMS

Business owners must realize there are no cookie-cutter backup systems. That's one of the problems with many IT providers in business today. Many of them, if not most of them, are approaching backup as a one-size-fits-all approach and they are selling based on price. This is great for my business because when I go into an organization that has a one-size-fits-all backup system, I simply ask, "Since you have all your data backed up to the cloud, what happens when Hurricane Sandy hits? How do you actually gain access to your 15 terabytes of data in the cloud?" Unfortunately, they usually don't know how they will retrieve it. I am then able to advise them what is needed to be able to retrieve their data in a timely fashion and mitigate their business risk.

WHAT NOT TO DO

Don't use the "back up everything" approach. When a business allows their data to grow without control, they aren't doing themselves a favor. Remember, the more data you have the more you have to backup.

Don't neglect to segment your backup. You need to prioritize the order in which you will need your data. If you segment your backups you can prioritize the restores.

Don't co-mingle the tier 1 data with the tier 2, 3 and 4 data. For example, you probably don't want to combine your financial data with your Word documents. Typically you will want to restore your financial data before Word documents.

Don't take the backup tape home. If you use a tape backup system, don't put it in the hands of even your most trusted employee. In many offices, someone like the secretary or another designated person becomes responsible for taking home the backup tape so it's not left in the office overnight. But what happens if the secretary loses the backup tape? What if the designated person leaves the tape in the car and the weather takes its toll on it and it can't be restored? Do you realize you are placing your entire business in the hands of a secretary who takes your backup tapes home at night?

HOW IMPORTANT IS YOUR DATA?

Backup is the second most important responsibility in IT; second only to maintaining the daily operation of your business. Keeping the day-to-day business running is clearly the most important activity. But if you don't have a backup of your data, nothing else will matter if your business is suddenly destroyed. Disaster is inevitable; it's just a matter of when. I know this because I live in the path of Hurricane Sandy. If you would have told me that type of storm would happen in my lifetime, I would have told you, "No way!" But it did, and many businesses were not prepared. Think about those people who had their backup tapes at home when their home was destroyed by the hurricane. Not only was their office inaccessible, but also they lost all their data because their backup tape was under nine feet of water.

How important is your data to you? One business owner with whom I talked was a victim of Hurricane Sandy and had no access to their building for ten days. That downtime cost them about $250,000 a day. They learned a valuable lesson about the importance of their data to the functioning of their business. They no longer have someone take the backup tapes home with them every day. The disaster put them in a completely different frame of mind when it comes to the value of their data. Unfortunately, many business owners don't think about how they will recover their data until they can't.

CONSIDER THE COST

When people look at backup they often focus primarily on the cost. They look at the cost of the server, the software, etc. and think that's the only cost involved. They don't consider the cost of lost data. Data backup is like an insurance policy. No one enjoys mailing a check to the insurance company, but those that have had their homes replaced by the insurance company are very thankful and don't feel bad when they pay their insurance premium. Their perspective changes as a result of their experience. It's much the same way for a business owner. They don't enjoy paying for the backup costs, but they are very glad to have their data restored promptly when disaster strikes.

We encourage our clients to backup to the cloud, to make a backup locally and to a remote site so they have multiple copies of their data. For example, one of my law firm clients has three offices. Their primary office is where their data center is located. For backup, we make a copy in their local office, a copy in their remote office and then an additional copy to the cloud. They are prepared for the next Hurricane Sandy and for real regional disasters. They have associated a cost specifically to not having access to their data. They know how much money it will cost them if they can't work for a day, or three days, or a week. That in turn places a value on their backup data.

HUMAN ERROR AND THE LOSS OF DATA

People overlook the fact that data loss is not usually due to big disasters; most of the time it's due to human error. It's Becky in accounting who accidently drags and drops a significant number of files into the trash folder and nobody realized it for three days. Human error is probably the biggest culprit to lost data and the one we see most. When we get calls saying something is wrong with the system because all the files in a certain directory disappeared, our investigation often reveals human error caused the issue which resulted in data loss.

Another cause of data loss is when employees leave either voluntarily or involuntarily. It's not uncommon for a departing employee to delete all the files. Or if a disgruntled employee wants to irritate his manager, he may move the files around to create at least temporary panic or disorientation.

GAME CHANGERS IN DATA BACKUP

An issue we often see is people wanting to recover previous versions of files. Because of the advancements in technology, we are now implementing systems that not only give our clients the backup of their data, but it also gives them previous versions of their data. For example, if a client created a budget file and at 4:30 p.m. says, "I really wish I had the budget file I created at 9:00 a.m.," we can easily retrieve the 9:00 a.m. data as well as 50 other versions of the file if needed. This is becoming a much requested item in today's business environment, and most of today's backup systems allow the end user to easily retrieve this data without having to depend on the IT department.

Another data backup game changer has been virtualization. Virtualization gives us a whole new backup opportunity which was impossible just a few short years ago. Five years ago, if you wanted to back up a server the way it is backed up now, it could take hours to make that happen. For example, many companies will close out a financial period and will want a pristine copy of that financial period. Before, this would mean the part of the business being reflected in this report will not operate for a short period of time until their systems were completely backed up. However, now with virtualization, the user can literally press a button to make a backup and three seconds later have an identical copy of that entire server. That backup can be used to continue making backups every so many minutes or hours and roll back to specific points in time to recover data. That is a huge advancement in technology!

Historically, a traditional backup meant that I make a copy of my data and dump it somewhere, but unless I had a specific server for the backup I couldn't actually do anything with it. It was just there. Now, with virtualization I can make a backup to the cloud or somewhere else. But, not only can I make a backup, I can actually make it run so it is more than a backup, it's actually a functional version of the data.

STEPS TO TAKE FOR EFFECTIVE BACKUP

In summary, here are the steps that a business should take when considering backup options.

1. Identify what you want to backup.
2. Prioritize the order in which you want your data backed up and recovered.

3. Determine the frequency of your backups. (e.g., daily, twice a day, hourly etc.)

4. Determine an acceptable amount of time to recover your data. (e.g., instantly, 4 hours, next business day, etc.)

5. Determine where you will store your data. (e.g., locally, remotely, cloud, etc.)

6. Test your backup system. (This is a point many business owners fail to do.)

Don't Go It Alone

One of the most important things to consider with whatever approach you use for data backup is to make sure you have some mechanism for real support. When problems arise, you don't want to be emailing someone to figure out how to get your data back. You want to be able to pick up the phone and call a qualified IT professional who has intimate knowledge of your backup system and the type of data being backed up. You need an IT professional most when you have a problem but don't have time to help them figure out how to retrieve data from a backup with which they are not familiar. You don't want to approach data backup alone. Make sure you have a support mechanism in place in the form of an IT provider.

About Carl

Carl A. Scalzo is the Chief Executive Officer of Online Computers and Communications, LLC. Since founding the company in 2012, he has built a dedicated team of over 40 employees in two locations. Carl is responsible for the management, development, and strategic direction of the company's technology systems and functions, while maintaining a strong, personal relationship with his clients, as well as his business partners and vendors.

Carl has more than 25 years of experience in strategic technology solutions for business and organizations throughout New York and New Jersey. He specializes in integrating the most advanced, secure, and reliable technology systems for his clients.

During his career, Carl has gained experience working with multiple business segments including health care facilities, schools, doctors' offices, legal offices, and Non-Profit organizations. His business reach extends through New York, New Jersey, Maryland, and Washington, D.C.

For more than two decades, he has assisted his clients in understanding how information technology can aid in furthering the success of their business. He has a deep understanding of the importance of business continuity, and how to further grow the success of a business or organization strictly through the use of technology.

With significant experience in financial fundraising software Blackbaud CRM, Carl has been responsible for the management of information systems and consulting services for many Non-Profit organizations. He was intimately involved in five of the largest Blackbaud CRM implementations throughout the country, and has been the Chair of the FTPI conference for the Federation system several times.

Carl is a regular presenter at conferences and trade shows. He has been featured in Newspapers such as *The New Jersey Jewish News*, and has received mentions in a number of volumes and other publications.

******

(Addendum follows on p.37)

ADDENDUM

Datto is the difference between downtime and uptime. When backup is not enough and downtime is not an option, Datto delivers continuity. Intelligent Business Continuity is the entire process, start to finish, that keeps a business' operations running. The elements of continuity are: Image-based backup, Hybrid cloud-based backup, Instant Virtualization, Superior Recovery Time Objective (RTO), and Incomparable Recovery Point Objective (RPO). If a piece is missing, it's not continuity, from the type of backup, instant virtualization to secure cloud, complete system recovery, all while maintaining the means to keep a business operational and open for business. Continuity is a key differentiator for businesses today.

datto

CHAPTER 4

BYOD (BRING YOUR OWN DEVICE) — WHY RESISTANCE IS FUTILE AND WHAT YOU NEED TO KNOW TO DEVELOP EFFECTIVE POLICIES IN YOUR WORK ENVIRONMENT

SCOTT GORCESTER

WHAT IS BYOD?

Most of us know the phrase – BYOB, where party invitations would use the term to let you know that if you wanted to drink, you had to "Bring Your Own Bottle." BYOD is the tech world equivalent meaning "Bring Your Own Device," referring to the policy of permitting or even encouraging employees to bring their personal mobile devices (laptops, tablets, smart phones, etc.) to the workplace. When I say resistance is futile in the title, I'm referring to the significant inroads this practice is making in the United States and international business worlds.

Approximately 75 percent of employees in high growth markets such as Brazil and Russia and close to 45 percent in developed markets are already using their own technology at work. This chapter provides you with a high level view of what you need to know to begin to develop your own BYOD policy.

In general the intention of a BYOD policy is the company subsidizes an employee's purchase of one or more devices, including mobile phones, notebooks, and tablets. These then belong to the employee and the employee takes on the responsibility to maintain them while the company provides tech support. I look at the BYOD practice as empowering and inspiring employees to be more productive by allowing them some control over the devices they use to do their jobs. Providing technical support for several different devices and varying platforms may be a challenge and is something to consider when building your company's BYOD plan. The most promising aspect of this new phenomenon is that employees ultimately become more productive as each individual is offered a choice that maximizes his or her comfort level and flexibility. It allows your staff to have a more personalized experience because they can continue to use systems they are comfortable with and don't have to switch to different platforms.

INITIAL CHALLENGES, RISKS AND THE IMPORTANCE OF BYOD POLICIES

The first challenge to enabling employees to bring their own devices is assuring they have suitable devices to perform their jobs. From my experience, the breakdown is that some employees have a device they are willing to use, others do not have a suitable device, and a third group may expect their employer to subsidize or outright purchase new devices. In a lot of cases, businesses are subsidizing the purchase of one or more user devices, and leaving it to the employee to make the final choice and complete the purchase. Setting clear guidelines for employees and insuring that the company communicates easy-to-follow instructions will insure success. To this end it's important to have strong policies in place governing this transaction that employees read, understand fully, and agree to as a condition of receiving this device. Consistency, efficiency, and workability are the keys to creating and maintaining an effective policy.

Another essential challenge that needs to be addressed in a detailed policy is how employees will connect their devices to the corporate system. Despite its growing popularity, BYOD is truly a double-edged sword. You want to empower and enable your employees with easy access to data, but it's critical to manage the significant risks of doing so. If you are not careful, it's possible to expose your company to great security risks. These risks may include loss of data, corruption of data, and unauthorized access.

One of the concerns that's easily overlooked by those new to BYOD is underestimating the number of devices that employees have or may use to access company data and email. You may think your employee is just using one or two devices to connect, but that person may also connect from a home PC, and various other devices. Fortunately, there are software applications and tools available that can help you discover what devices are connected to your system. Often when we perform a review of a customer's mail server, we find significantly more devices than expected; it is not uncommon that a client might expect there are 20 devices connecting but in reality there may be 100 or more. It's important to invest in software and services that allow you to scan your system to see who and what is connecting to your sensitive corporate data.

Another potential problem is that once an employee connects a phone, laptop or tablet to the company's email server, secure information that's in the company's system ends up on that device, and may be viewable by family members or friends of the employee who might use the device. Data breaches, data loss and leakage can happen when devices are not properly secured.

In light of these concerns it's important that companies develop sound policies to mitigate such risks. Additionally, it's necessary to provide ongoing training for employees that reinforces proper behavior. Having a policy is great but it can't be something which exists in a notebook somewhere and is only loosely adhered to. Because of the sensitivity of the information, strict policies needs to be effectively applied and followed.

In the IT business, we see crazy things in the field every day. An employee lost an iPad; the good news is, he had a lock on it, the bad news is that the key to the lock is written on a sticker somewhere on the device. This is where constant training and reinforcement comes in. Use worst-case scenario examples in your training and create a sequence of consequences as part of your policies, including written warnings, for employees who violate these policies.

Here's a crazy tidbit that illustrates the importance of addressing data risk. Personal devices can now be subpoenaed in court as part of the legal discovery process. The people and companies involved in civil and criminal litigation may be forced to submit their personal phones, tablets and laptops for analysis. This creates a potential risk of an employee's personal information being caught up in corporate litigation. That means these investigators can potentially see texts, chats and personal or corporate email that may be sensitive in nature. When it comes to BYOD devices, I personally believe the pros outweigh the cons, but if you are not effectively managing the cons, you open yourself up to a host of potentially serious risks.

IMPORTANT TIPS TO REDUCE BYOD RISKS

1. Focus on Employee Mobile Device Management

The most important aspect of allowing employees to connect their devices to the company systems is ensuring proper security. Security concerns are more than just protecting your data and systems from unauthorized access, they also include ensuring the safety of your data from damage or other threats of data loss. There are numerous tools you can use to secure devices such as smartphones and tablets. These tools will allow you to control or analyze your system to ensure that devices are connecting using proper passwords, data encryption, and other forms of data protection. These types of devices when connected to a corporate network can pose a threat of infecting that network with a virus if both systems are not properly protected. When you allow employees to connect their personal devices to the company network, it is also wise to provide them with company-managed antivirus and anti-malware programs. Providing this service ensures that the company has full control of software that keeps systems and data safe.

There are various cloud-based services and software you can install on your network to assist with providing authorized access to company data, without risk of it getting out into the wild. Special virtualization technologies, such as Citrix desktop virtualization, which virtualizes applications and desktops and allows employees to access them from their personal mobile devices, provide companies the ability to keep data from ending up on the employees' personal devices. Employee Mobile Device Management isn't about locking down access entirely, it's about mitigating security risks by having the ability to control the device and what it can access. The way I look at security: it is a balancing act to prevent loss or corruption while making it easy for authorized users to access what they need, when they need it. It would be great if we could lock everything in a safe, but that isn't practical. It is, however, important to determine where the risks may lie and provide appropriate security measures and continuously monitor for potential threats.

A big issue when employees utilize mobile phones for company business is giving out personal numbers to customers and prospects. Intentionally or not customers become trained to contact the employees via their personal phone numbers rather than using the main corporate office number, and this becomes a critical issue when an employee leaves the company. If over the course of time 100 sales people leave the company, and 200 of their customers and prospects had only the employees' personal contact numbers, that's 20,000 customers, and potential customers, which are at risk of being re-directed to the competition. Generally, it should be policy that employees should not give out their personal phone numbers to customers. This can be enforced by blocking Caller ID or routing calls in a manner such that the corporate phone number shows up when an employee places a call.

Though Employee Mobile Device Management may vary depending on the devices and risks involved, one thing everyone should do is enable the remote wipe feature or software on the phone, tablet or laptop. It is a management tool which will allow you, in the case where a device with sensitive data is lost or stolen, to destroy data on that device if it's turned on. In many cases this software can even locate the device.

2. Using Cloud Technology, or "Sandboxing"

Once you have the inbound threats taken care of, the next way to protect yourself is understanding how to protect the data that's being accessed. Using various cloud, and other forms of virtualization technology, allows employees to bridge the powerful gap between having access to the data they need, while still preventing the leakage of data. The increasingly sophisticated world of cloud technology has facilities for this, or you can subscribe to services offering what my company, VirtualQube, does. Our hosted private cloud solutions are designed and built in accordance with the best practice recommendations for Citrix Service Providers. Citrix allows employee access to corporate data and applications while preventing the data from actually reaching the employee's physical device. Employees can run their productivity applications on their devices but when they shut down the devices nothing is left behind. A term we use for this concept is "Sandboxing". By leveraging this type of virtualization technology, you empower employees by providing them with access to an endless array of compute resources which they can access from their own devices, but you can still prevent the possibility of important data leaking outside of your system.

3. Understand All Related Legal Issues

Obviously, the specific BYOD policies you create will be driven and governed by the industry you are in. If you are in the legal or medical profession, you may be dealing with government compliance requirements that will have an enormous impact on how you develop and maintain corporate security policies. Medical organizations were recently forced to put specific policies in play related to requirements for electronic medical records software. If you're dealing with vendors providing credit card transactions, there are very specific guidelines, which must be tied to your policies in order to ensure that you protect sensitive customer data.

4. Setting Expectations

When you allow your employees to bring their own devices, which will have access to corporate data, you will avoid many headaches if you establish an "acceptable use" policy that must be agreed upon in writing before the employees are allowed to connect their devices to the network. In order to protect corporate data from theft, an acceptable use policy might include anything from limiting the device's access by other people, not allowing certain activities to be performed on the device, requiring secure passwords of seven or more characters, having corporate approved anti-virus and anti-malware protection on the device, and incredibly important is accepting the company policy that if the employee leaves the company under less than favorable terms, personal devices may automatically be wiped including personal data. While it may seem obvious to tell employees not to have any illegal content on the device, it's not as uncommon as you might think to run across corporate-used devices with illegally-downloaded content. To encourage more productivity during business hours, many companies will also desire to limit access to shopping sites, social media sites such as Facebook, Twitter, and Pinterest – just to name a few. A brief review of employee devices will often reveal large amounts of website access to non-company related content.

5. Social Media Monitoring

Every company makes unique decisions about their employees and social media. Some say we should never allow any social media activity on personal or corporate-owned devices which are used for business. I think this is ultimately too restrictive and impractical. There are numerous possible benefits for using social media sites to do business, but on the other hand, we all know Facebook, Twitter, and the like can become a huge distraction. The solution, as with all aspects of BYOD, might be to allow social media but provide acceptable use guidelines that employees must adhere to. I ask that employees limit personal use of social media during the workday. If I'm going to allow you to use it, I ask you not to abuse it. It's the same with using a company phone for personal calls. A few minutes to arrange to have a child picked up or other important personal business is fine. There are many different ways to monitor employee use, from being able to view their screens, cameras in the office, and of course, there are many different types of specialized software which will monitor their activities.

Your employees should know in advance what to expect if they are discovered participating in behaviors they agreed to avoid. Generally, if they know there are consequences, such as warnings, which could ultimately lead to termination, they won't violate the rules. Setting proper expectations up front lowers the risk of security and activity breaches. From my experience, I can say that the worst thing a company can do is to allow a BYOD free-for-all, allowing unrestricted or unmanaged use of employee devices, i.e., don't allow anarchy to prevail.

In Star Trek, the phrase "Resistance is futile!" is part of the standard message used by the Borg, the fictional alien antagonists, when they encounter an alien race they intend to assimilate into their collective. As BYOD becomes likewise an inevitable part of the corporate milieu, the road from being intimidated to embracing it is made easier if you understand the risks and set realistic expectations for yourself and your employees.

About Scott

Scott Gorcester is an IT visionary and entrepreneur. Scott, Founder and Chief Executive Officer, founded VirtualQube in 2012, and has been defining the company strategy, refining the products and developing a strong partnership program. He is a seasoned businessman and skilled IT architect, technician and trainer. He and his team designed and built the technology stacks in use by VirtualQube today.

Prior to founding VirtualQube, he was president of Moose Logic, an IT company he founded in 1994. Moose Logic was one of the original 100 Citrix resellers and Scott was one of the first people to use the technology to provide early cloud computing solutions for clients. Moose Logic received accolades for numerous accomplishments including three consecutive years on the *Puget Sound Business Journal's* "Fast Growing Companies in Washington State" list. It was also the #1 reseller of Citrix Software in the United States in the first quarter of 1999, beating out companies four to five times its size.

Scott entered the technology industry in 1991 as a sales executive with Applied Computer Sciences. He is an accomplished race car driver, winning the International Conference of Sports Car Clubs' "Super Production Over 5 Liters" (SPO) Championship in 2002 and setting a course-qualifying record for Improved Touring "E" class in 2006. Scott was accepted into the "Sports Car Club of America" (SCCA) Pro series in 2006. He is not currently competing, but he continues to hone his driving skills on a track and racing simulator. In addition, he is working on a program to encourage young people to become better drivers. Scott understands the importance of a well-designed machine and applies the same attention-to-detail and integrity to his clients' business systems as he does to his race cars.

CHAPTER 5

THE FUTURE OF YOUR SMB IN THE CLOUD

BY KARL BURNS

If you've got a small business and you are already embracing the tenets and benefits of using the "Cloud," you may already be aware of a number of organizational options in front of you. But if you haven't gone down this path yet, as my uncle says, "Take good notes."

I once attended one of the premiere Entrepreneurship events in the country hosted by Wake Forest University. The day-long competition puts teams of entrepreneurs into a real-life scenario; convince an investor to take a meeting with you during a 60 second elevator ride to the 44th floor of an office building in Winston Salem, North Carolina. While providing an overview of the event, one professor was keen to say "If you cannot explain the business you are in 20 words or less, you don't understand what business you are in." I would take that concept one step further when thinking about technology in SMBs: If you spend more than 30 minutes a day solving technology issues, you are not a business person but a part-time technology staff member. This is where the cloud really starts to help business owners. In the following pages we will look at the impacts according to this framework:

GENERAL BENEFITS OF CLOUD

Embracing the cloud as the support structure for your business opens new doors for your company. Some of the most talked about benefits are bending/lowering the cost curve and moving capital investments to operating costs, making IT expenses more predictable. The cloud should also be embraced for the benefits of an increase in technology maturity as well as the reduction in business risk it provides. One of those risks is the underlying technology. Cloud vendors leverage the most tested, robust technologies available supported by best-practices of IT support. The cloud service industry has grown in scale to now offer SMBs a competitive price, and included in that price are the best practices of the industry. (It's rare that a SMB has the maturity to implement every IT best practice.) There is also a reduction in risk from employees. For instance, employees cannot sabotage technology assets accidentally or with malice when those assets are in the cloud. And there's no chance of hardware disappearing overnight either. Another benefit is business resilience provided with "Fail-Over" and "Follow-Me Data" capabilities because the cloud has built-in disaster recovery plans already in place. This provides SMBs and their employees the ability to continue to work when connectivity outages occur, which they will. In conclusion, the cost benefits of the cloud make it a simple decision, but the softer benefits of continuity and maturity are where SMBs can experience significant increases in business value.

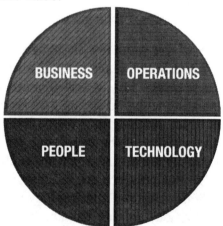

Business Impact Framework

OPERATIONAL IMPACTS

The cloud enables new business organizational models. Before we explore these new opportunities, let's level-set on some observations about SMBs. Historically SMBs are built on the backs of go getters. Employees at SMBs execute loosely defined processes to make the firm money, whether it's sales, order processing, customer management, service delivery, etc. Cash costs are watched religiously, and investments are infrequent and not always planned. Employees are often hired by happenstance, with little to no time to train and develop. Some new hires are chosen for their hunger and determination over a candidate with more industry experience. These new hires are also cheaper which fits into the SMB's cost conscious mindset. A go-getter attitude is more valued than that of a team player because SMBs have not had the technology structure, nor the process-focused discipline to support the growth and development of employees. SMBs rarely have the internal resources available to standardize end-to-end processes. Most of the time, processes are championed by a single employee with no oversight, resulting in inconsistency (and often re-work) across the organization. This also inhibits business intelligence and any performance measurement. When a SMB uses cloud technology to support their business, it can answer the un-stated need for toll gates and handoffs, resulting in reduced re-work and increased efficiency. In order for the business benefits to really take hold, there is a need for clear communication from SMB owners touting the need for process consistency, and the need for performance measurement. Because of the cloud, SMBs will have the tools necessary to make this a reality.

With a consistent, process driven technology support structure, the need for business users to drive entire processes will diminish. But the need for specific processes will continue to grow. Similar to how the cloud moves technology costs from a capital discussion to an operating cost discussion, the cloud-enabled SMB will have the ability to have 3rd parties deliver low-impact, but time-consuming business services. This ability is already being practiced by large enterprises, and the benefits can be staggering. The drivers of this savings will be labor arbitrage, economies of scale and third party specialization, which reduces time to completion and increases accuracy. SMBs will need to measure and incentivize business outcomes both internally and externally with their vendors. While not a technology cost savings, this opportunity to lower the cost of operations will be readily available to cloud-enabled SMBs.

PEOPLE IMPACTS

Specifically looking at the IT work force of a cloud enabled SMB, there will likely be changes to the IT staff as well as business staff. For instance you will not need technology skills to install, change, or retire network infrastructure. You will not need technology skills to execute prolonged back up activities and processes. You will not need IT resources to build and re-image computers and other user-facing assets. With the right cloud provider you can have technology support completely managed by a ticket with predictability, traceability, and SLA-driven outcomes. This will lower the cost of service delivery, allow for performance measurement and allow for pro active maintenance to reduce service outages. You will no longer need to worry about the hiring, replacing or firing IT talent and you will no longer need to worry about what the IT person does or knows. While the SMB will not require IT project delivery skills, the management of service delivery and vendors will be of critical importance. By leveraging the cloud capabilities, enterprise maturity will immediately be in place for your company. For instance, disaster recovery plans will already be tested and implemented, and infrastructure refresh and planning will already be in full-swing. The Cloud support structure will already have fail-over procedures in place, and there will be limited ability for an employee error to interrupt the business. With fail-over capabilities, the abilities to see and understand processes, and a newfound reliance on ticketing tools for support management, SMB employees will likely experience an increase in trust across the organization. The value of trust can never be understated.

TECHNOLOGY TRANSITION

While there is a reduction in some IT skills historically required by SMBs, there are new skills required by SMBs to operate effectively with cloud support technology. There will be an increase in need for project management skills. There will also be an increase in need for vendor management. There will be an increase in the need for all technology employees to have more business acumen and knowledge. In fact, Deloitte recently published a report in the Wall Street Journal also identifying the increased demands for high end software development (usability, custom reporting, etc.) Making sense of high volumes of data, including how to organize and analyze large data stores, will also be increasingly important. Also essential in IT operations is a clear understanding of the impact of IT systems on business processes. This requires a broad understanding of the systemic relationships between specific IT activities and the business activities they support. IT workers can no longer hide behind "the wall", but have to be true business partners.

The "Cloud" will undoubtedly cause a breakdown of traditional relationships between IT and the business. Cloud adoption will likely be the source of unpredictable competition and cause turbulence within IT organizations as they seek to reskill themselves and their IT professionals to support the new model. However, in the end, most enterprises will benefit from the increased level of business value and opportunity that is a result of the cloud climate change.

In a cloud supported SMB, the level of IT expertise can decrease and that's okay. With a cloud supported IT structure, SMBs will no longer need to keep up with all the latest technology trends. SMBs will already get upgraded hardware as part of their support because automatic refreshes will already be priced into their contracts. Enterprise-quality software will be available by immediate demonstration (or pilot program), and movement across platforms will be easier with standard data storage policies and structures. You may experience line-of-business leaders everywhere bypassing IT departments to get applications from the cloud (also known as software as a service, or SaaS) and paying for them like they would a magazine subscription. And when the service is no longer required, they can cancel that subscription with no equipment left unused in the corner. This should not be seen as usurping power or responsibility from the IT organization, but a more expedient and streamlined way to implement software to generate business value.

SMBs will no longer suffer through expensive software implementations. Historically these implementations are hindered by a lack of documentation and a lack of business buy-in. The promise to SMBs of a best-in-class solution was rarely achieved due to lackluster change management (if any), no change of business process and reduced solution capabilities in order to save costs. In a cloud supported IT structure, software selection can be made rapidly with short puppy dog tests by users instead of the months long cross-functional committee analysis currently practiced. This change in software selection methodology will improve user acceptance, will increase the business ideas for improvement, will enable side by side comparisons and will offer easy integration with standard data sets. Another benefit of the cloud supported SMB is that international expansion will be easier than ever. With an increase in the support SMBs can provide remote employees, the opportunity to hire foreign talent will also increase, which will increase the number of markets available to a SMB. This hiring of international talent will be made even easier by frequent work-from-home practices in other countries, reducing the workplace expense during expansion. There is a growing supply of English speaking business people who can help your company throughout the world. Just in case, translation services are more readily available than ever, and Google's translator is still a product being refined (and free). The limiting factors facing SMBs will fall to the wayside as cloud-enabled SMBs grow over the coming years.

BUSINESS TRANSITION

As cloud technologies standardize, these technology resource costs will continue to decline. The decline in cost will be the result of an increase in the standardization of skills, an increase in the standardization of processes, and an increase in the software capabilities to manage technology. These will be met by an increase in the supply of technology skills from workers all over the world. There will be an increased need for MSP services but SMBs will no longer face million dollar IT refreshes every five years. What do you think you would do with that extra cash every five years? Likewise, what would you do with the extra time not spent on RFPs or planning which hardware to purchase? The SMB technology needs can be met by an increase in new MSP services, which are high skill and high value. MSPs will have the opportunity to sell skills which deliver software development layers on enterprise CRMs, Java and .NET skills for hire, big-data analytics for hire, and industry expertise / consulting. The main takeaway so far is that no business owner or executive should ever have to know how to install a network service. Once supported by the "cloud," they never will again.

SMBs were built with dedicated no-holds barred service delivery because the infrastructure wasn't available to support the business at every growth stage. With cloud-support, the SMB infrastructure will make new opportunities available; opportunities formerly reserved for the largest enterprises. As the biggest software vendors enter the SMB markets, the prices charged to SMBs will decline to meet their budgetary concerns. At first, enterprise tools will offer more functionality than SMBs require, but the value equation might convince SMBs to go this direction as the industry experiences the typical flight to quality. The standardization of data will occur simultaneously, making it easier to transition on/off various platforms. The flight to quality will be the fences established brands build around their customers as they separate themselves within the lower-tiered markets as they have with enterprise customers. Price vs. functionality will continue to be the trade-off for SMBs, but the equation will not be so drastic. It will also be an earlier adoption by SMBs of enterprise solutions in order to decrease the number of changes a SMB may endure over its life. This increase in the usage of enterprise tools by SMBs will raise the skills required by SMBs and extend the user base enormously.

SKILLS FOR THE "NEW" SMB

Above I have outlined the way I think the future of SMBs will occur based on my experience and knowledge. I would like to take this opportunity to point out where SMBs will need to skill-up. The areas to focus on even more are business planning, talent management, organizational excellence and leadership communications.

PLANNING STILL CRITICAL

Even with an improved maturity in technology and business support, SMBs will still need disciplined planning methodologies. For example businesses will need to be clear about their product strategies, including target markets, unmet needs, competitive whitespace, products/feature bundles, product evolution, real-options for products and strategic alliances. Businesses will also need to methodically plan their expansion, whether this expansion is organic (self-funded expansion over the long term), inorganic (outside investments for rapid scale expansion) or via strategic alliance. The cloud enabled SMB will have access to more internal and external data than ever before but will need to be able to see the opportunities amongst the noise of the market.

TALENT STILL CRITICAL

With a different mix of skills and additional support structure from cloud technology, talent management is still critical. SMBs will continue to face the challenge of hiring the "right" people, and will have to be flexible about training and development. SMBs will also be rigid and firm when talent decisions must be made. The Cloud enabled SMB will have the data needed to provide accurate rewards for employees. The SMB will need to provide the right incentives to maximize the contribution of its employees. Some recommendations for SMBs are:

provide a balance of organizational and individual rewards, provide a balance between monetary reward and recognition award, and provide timely and constant feedback for training and development.

MATURITY STILL CRITICAL

With the newfound capabilities of a cloud supported technology structure, SMBs still need to get their processes stabilized. There will continue to be a need for documented processes to support training and development. The opportunities to measure the firm's performance and efficiencies in things other than sales will not be available until the right toll-gates and metrics are in place.

COMMUNICATION MORE CRITICAL

There will still be a need to communicate consistently across the organization and there will continue to be a need to measure YoY changes in order to:

1) determine performance

2) measure improvement

3) set goals and incentivize behavior

While these organizational stability projects are taking place, the SMB leadership will still need to clearly articulate business objectives for the entire organization. Communication will be even more critical but the organization will have the data integrity to effectively measure department and individual KPIs. Communication from SMB leadership must tie the business vision back to these organizational and individual KPIs. In a cloud supported SMB, leadership communication will still be the most important contributor to your success.

IN CONCLUSION

The cloud will provide future SMBs with more opportunities than ever before, but these are only tools in the grand scheme of business. Getting the right people into the organization, and inspiring them to perform, rewarding that performance, and being flexible enough to change when appropriate will be the hallmarks of the SMBs.

About Karl

Karl Burns is the Chief Strategy Officer of VirtualQube. Since joining the firm, he has led initiatives focused on re-vamping the go-to-market strategy and operations, increasing organizational maturity, decreasing cost of service and scaling operations. Karl brings an enterprise discipline and approach to organizational development and also a financial acumen to assess business strategy (including acquisitions). He is also a steward of the VirtualQube culture, leading workshops which promote the mission and values of the firm.

Before VirtualQube, Karl worked in management consulting for both technology and new product development. He has led programs to improve internal business processes, develop technology roadmaps, design and implement e-commerce portals (financial services), re-design organizational structures, determine portfolio roadmaps, develop implementation plans for new businesses and their supporting technologies, and align products and services to customer engagement to drive incremental revenue. Karl's deep finance background helps clients focus on the economic logic of options available and facilitate prioritization across a large set of competing initiatives. Karl has experience in financial services, telecom, insurance, retail and manufacturing – including Fortune 500 clients like Best Buy, AT&T, Ally Bank, Nike, Nationwide, DISH Network, Xerox, HP, Bank of New York-Mellon, and Citigroup.

Prior to this experience, Karl worked for PNC Bank in the mutual fund services group in Boston. While serving as an account executive, Karl managed service delivery generating more than $2.4 million in annual revenue. In this role, Karl helped transform their external website, improved internal processes to lower the cost of service delivery, and championed a project with a marquee client to reduce annual compliance spend by 70% within the first year. Karl also worked on new product development definitions and beta-testing of new web services (SaaS).

Karl received a BA in Economics from Texas A&M University Mays School of Business in 1999, and completed his MBA at Wake Forest University in 2008. He received the "Babcock Leadership Award" for the student who best displayed the core characteristics of Wake Forest: Management, Scholarship, Integrity, and Leadership. He now fund-raises for the Vanderbilt-Ingram Cancer Center with the "Young Ambassadors" group, which has raised more than $250,000 over the past three years. This group awards discovery grants to individual medical researchers fighting cancer.

CHAPTER 6

eCOMMERCE:
WHY START AND PIECES
OF THE PUZZLE

BY BEN ORTH

As an SMB (Small/Medium Business) Owner you likely fall into one of three areas when you think of eCommerce:

1. You haven't tried as it appears difficult, expensive, etc.

2. Your business has eCommerce experience but perhaps hasn't met its goals or expectations.

3. Your eCommerce business is successful.

If you identify with either of the first two, help is at hand. Let's explore why you should consider eCommerce, places to start, and the pieces of the puzzle to match up. If you've been successful, congratulations! Stay with me because a review of the fundamentals is a great way to remain successful.

Stripped to its essence, electronic commerce, commonly known as eCommerce, occurs when the buying and selling of products or services is conducted over electronic systems such as the Internet and other computer networks. While it has many different definitions and elements, let's talk about the idea of shopping carts and customer service portals and how they can help your business.

When people think of eCommerce, large concerns like Amazon, Walmart, or Office Depot come to mind. These are known as B2C or Business to Consumer. A larger part of eCommerce is B2B, or Business to Business. The contrast of B2B versus B2C opportunities is significant. Forrester Research, Inc., a leading independent research firm, forecasts 2013 B2B transactions will reach $559 billion versus B2C with $252 billion.[1] In addition to capturing your piece of the eCommerce "pie", there are a number of customer and company benefits that are powerful motivations for you to invest in eCommerce.

EXTERNAL FACTORS BRINGING CHANGE

As SMB owners with successful eCommerce experience will attest, eCommerce is a *competitive advantage*. What are the warning signs you may be at a competitive disadvantage without it? Answering "Yes" to questions like:

- Are customers requesting eCommerce?
- Do you have key customers requiring it?

So, why this change?

First, your customers are as short staffed as you. They may view it a waste of their resources to play phone tag, wait on hold to place orders that don't require order handling expertise or get answers to product questions.

Second, with the proliferation of personal devices accelerating the speed of life, many folks want to do things at their convenience on their schedule, not your business' schedule.

Lastly, the convenience of online bill payment in our personal lives is extending to business operations, creating a need to enable payment of open accounts with the convenience of electronic checks.

To survive the recent period of economic downturn, many companies downsized. As economic conditions improve and expand, many companies will face the decision of hiring additional staff to accommodate growth and improve customer satisfaction – or automating where they can within their businesses.

---

1 http://www.forrester.com/Key+Trends+In+B2B+eCommerce+For+2013/fulltext/-/E-RES82102

Competitive Advantage
A common misconception is that offering a lower price is the best competitive advantage. But in today's business world, competitive advantage may have little to do with price. Ease of doing business with you, product availability, a consistent buying experience, accuracy and depth of product information and accepted payment methods are other factors that weigh heavily in a customer's buying decision.

For example, a 2012 white paper by Hybris Software "2012 State of B2B eCommerce" noted that 8 out of 10 B2B procurers would opt for a supplier that offers online ordering over a supplier that offers only a printed catalog.[2]

Offering your customers an easy-to-use eCommerce solution will give you a competitive advantage in many of these areas.

YOUR CUSTOMERS AND YOU BENEFIT

Your customers (existing and future) and you, the SMB owner, benefit from a properly defined and executed eCommerce strategy that incorporates a shopping cart and customer service portal. Here's how:

- Your customers may, at their convenience any time of day or night:
  - Check pricing and availability
  - Place orders without having to call
  - Receive notification of order fulfillment
  - Track their order and shipping status
  - Use their previous orders as a basis for re-ordering
  - View and reprint their invoices and payment information
  - View and pay open invoices
- You may:
  - Gain efficiencies to handle more business with existing staff – no hiring right away to meet new demand
  - Free up experienced staff to handle situations that require their expertise, not simple minutia

---

2 http://hybris.com/en/downloads/whitepaper-state-of-b2b-e-commerce

- Increase sales volume through cross-sell and upsell item suggestions right on your website
- Build customer loyalty and satisfaction as you make it easier for them to do business with you

B2C VS B2B

Before tackling places to start and the pieces of the puzzle for eCommerce, let's consider what separates B2C and B2B in eCommerce.

While there are many similarities between them, two components of their business models provide the most defining differences.

- B2C eCommerce allows customers to purchase anonymously. The only requirement to buy is an electronic form of payment.
- In B2B the account is established by the seller.

Why the distinction?

Most distributors' and many manufacturers' business models match the B2B eCommerce because their business processes include one or more of the following:

- Offer discounted or net payment terms
- Discount or price structures based upon customer classes or types
- Sell only to qualified or authorized dealers
- Maintain exclusive geographic sales territories
- Product distribution subject to regulatory governance
- Sales tax exemption tracking and reporting

A note of caution here – With the recent economic challenges, some businesses look to sell their products and services to any market or customer group that will buy. Such a business strategy can make an eCommerce strategy and implementation very challenging because it likely includes B2C and B2B eCommerce.

PLACES TO START

You've decided to invest in eCommerce. Your next response is likely "Where do I start?" You start as you would with any new business strategy – research, become knowledgeable, and seek experienced advice.

This does not infer that you should or need to become an eCommerce expert. You want to gain enough knowledge to be able to ask intelligent questions and engage in meaningful discussions, so you can select a specific eCommerce solution that matches your strategy and business needs.

Of course, there's a wealth of Internet information, some accurate and helpful, some not so much. It can be a beginning but should not be the only source.

A trusted friendly competitor's eCommerce experience is a great place to gain tips as to what worked best for their situation, what they would do differently and the actual benefits achieved for their customers and themselves.

Industry trade associations for your business type are a valuable source. They have the resources and the mission to engage experts that bring topical information to improving members' businesses – eCommerce being a current topic of interest. Industry trade forums, webinars and publications can be a source of information as well.

The software publisher or its local representative for the line of business (LOB) solution that you use for order processing and fulfilment, inventory procurement or production, and related accounting and financial functions can be the most important resource – **if** you're confident that the LOB solution closely matches the needs of your business today, will scale as you grow the number and size of orders, and enable your business processes to support needs from the growth.

If you are **not** confident that your LOB solution meets the needs of your business today or its future growth, it's time to stop and address this central core of your business operation. There's no point spending resources to gain new business with eCommerce that you won't be able handle successfully and efficiently.

As you address this LOB solution deficiency, you'll likely encounter the acronym ERP (Enterprise Resource Planning). As an SMB owner, think LOB solutions when ERP is used. Remember that matching your business model, processes and needs to an appropriate LOB or ERP solution is the goal for addressing this deficiency, regardless of what it's called.

PIECES OF THE PUZZLE

During your research and quest for knowledge, you've encountered at least some of the pieces of the eCommerce puzzle. Key pieces include:

- B2C or B2B strategy
- Do-it-yourself or utilize experienced expertise
- Build the solution or use a commercial product that closely matches your needs
- Stand-alone solution, loosely coupled or integrated with your LOB/ERP solution
- Mind the details

SHOULD I DO IT MYSELF?

A quick Internet search of "ecommerce tools" yields thousands of options. So you may be tempted to do it yourself, engage your neighbor's college kid who has developed websites, or contract with an online firm advertising they do websites.

A question akin to "Should I do it myself?" is "Should I construct my business' office expansion myself?" The answer to both is that specialized skills, knowledge and expertise are required.

Building and implementing an eCommerce solution requires not only technical skills but expertise in security, and the ability to understand your business model and needs. You want to locate someone with expertise that can help you address specific concerns, and who can take control of managing and making sure that all of the i's are dotted and t's crossed. You don't want to get your system up and then realize there's a big piece missing or it doesn't support your business needs.

STANDALONE OR CONNECTING TO YOUR LOB SOLUTION

As your research likely found, eCommerce solutions fall into three broad categories in regards to your LOB solution:

- Standalone
- Loosely coupled to your LOB solution
- Tightly integrated with your LOB solution

Say you are a distributor with a narrow market niche and sell only a few dozen different items from stocked items. With minimal effort you can enter the product information and attach product images and establish pricing rules. You may be able to utilize a simple standalone eCommerce solution that collects orders and makes them available for you to re-enter into your LOB solution. Typically, standalone eCommerce solutions are provided as an online service for a monthly fee. Problem solved!

The SMB owner with a business that sells to hundreds or thousands of business customers, has complex pricing structures, and hundreds or thousands of items finds themself with a dilemma. The standalone eCommerce solution does not provide efficiencies needed to handle entry and maintenance of customer and item information in two separate systems or re-entry of orders from eCommerce into their LOB solution for fulfillment. To gain these efficiencies, a loosely coupled or a tightly integrated eCommerce solution must be considered.

Loosely-coupled systems gain some daily operation efficiencies because they generally eliminate manual re-entry of orders between your eCommerce solution and your LOB solution. Efficiency and information accuracy are likely gained from the elimination of manual updating of some product information such as quantity available. An eCommerce solution loosely coupled to an LOB is accomplished with one or more exports of information from one system and then imported into the other. The export/import process has to be initially configured and tested. For day-to-day operations, the export/import process may need to run manually, the results checked, and any exceptions or errors handled manually. Information timeliness is improved over standalone systems.

You gain the most benefits with an eCommerce solution tightly integrated with your LOB solution. The tight integration is accomplished with computer program to program communication through standardized interface points called API's or Application Program Interface. The API's may need to be configured and tested or may have specific selections that can be chosen based upon the LOB solution. The software publisher or their preferred partners are the best sources for tightly integrated eCommerce solutions for a specific LOB solution.

With tightly integrated eCommerce and LOB solutions, you gain the highest operational and maintenance efficiencies. Real time information updates (synchronization) between the systems ensure information in both systems is up to date and accurate.

MIND THE DETAILS

Successful selection of an eCommerce solution for your business model and needs must consider a number of details. Those with successful eCommerce strategies know to not assume that all eCommerce solutions are created equal. They recognize that minding the details is a key piece of the puzzle. Details include:

- Account creation and maintenance – who can create and change what information
- Product information – item id, short and long description, images, technical specifications, UPC
- Quantity – single or multiple units of measure
- Availability – available, actual quantity, by location
- Product attributes – size, color, weight, dimensions
- Product configuration/component options
- Pricing – quantity breaks, discount based, cost markup, customer class, contractual, promotion codes, promotional start/end dates
- Delivery and shipping – carrier choices, pricing
- Sales tax calculation and reporting
- Payment methodologies – credit and debit cards, private cards, electronic check, on account
- Payment processors – match with payment methodologies and processors for LOB
- Multicurrency
- Multilingual

COMMON MISTAKES TO AVOID

Two common mistakes frequently take a first time eCommerce solution off course.

When reviewing specific solutions, it's easy to get overwhelmed with information and inundated with all of the fancy features. Don't get lost in the complexity and bells and whistles. Your focus should always be on a solution that matches your essential business model and needs.

Another mistake occurs for some SMB owners when they think their businesses are so unique that they decide or become swayed when reviewing solutions that significant customization is required or a custom system is the only way to implement their eCommerce solution. If the customization becomes the focus, significant and unexpected financial investment may be required. Additionally the "go live" date can get pushed out to the future again and again. This only delays the benefits of an eCommerce strategy for your customer and you.

WRAPPING UP – MATCHING YOUR eCOMMERCE WITH TRADITIONAL BACK OFFICE SYSTEMS

As we discussed, the key area in terms of efficiency and accuracy is the integration of your eCommerce solution with existing back office systems. Most likely, even if you're doing eCommerce, you are also still taking orders the way you always have, via phone, email, and fax. Companies rarely cut off these other venues no matter how excited they are about eCommerce, so it's important to work towards seamless integration between your traditional way of taking orders and your eCommerce solution.

Everything you do in eCommerce needs to mesh with your overall business model, processes and needs.

About Ben

Ben Orth is the founder and CEO of Keystone Solutions, Inc., a technology firm located in the Kansas City area that thrives on solving tough eCommerce, ERP, and IT challenges for SMB business owners.

Keystone specializes in technology implementation services, business process refinement, project management, training, custom programming and ongoing support for the implemented technology systems.

Ben fell in love with computer programming and technology at an early age and strives to remain on the forefront of technology. Before starting Keystone Solutions, he worked for a municipal utility to develop and implement systems to move their manual operations into the computer age. He spent more than a decade improving and developing computer applications, leading development teams and migrating operations from mainframe to mainframe.

Ben is motivated by his passion for getting to the root of the problem. He loves to analyze his client's existing systems and help them gain efficiency and improve business resource utilization by finding and implementing the right technology solution.

That's why he's worked extensively with the types of operational and financial applications that make a business owner's life easier. From accounting applications, including billing, accounts payable and receivable, payroll, and general ledger with financial statements, to operational applications, including inventory, purchasing and order entry and fulfillment, to CRM and manufacturing applications, he can match the people, processes and technology, so the owner can get back to doing what they do best, running their business.

Recently his experiences and those of peers inspired Ben to lead development of eCommERPbridge™ for TRAVERSE® to meet today's challenges of eCommerce that face owners of distribution and manufacturing businesses.

Ben is also an active participant and member of, and facilitator for, several technology service provider business owner peer groups.

A Kansas native, Ben and his wife and business partner Teri have been married for more than forty years. Ben also enjoys both flower and vegetable gardening and loves to vacation in the Colorado Rockies while visiting his son Mike, who also works in the IT industry.

CHAPTER 7

HOW VoIP (VOICE OVER INTERNET PROTOCOL) IS TRANSFORMING THE TELECOMMUNICATIONS INDUSTRY AND THE WAY WE DO BUSINESS

BY DAVID WOLF

EXPLAINING THE BASICS: COPPER OUT, FIBER OPTICS IN

Chances are that if you're not already using VoIP for your business, you've at least heard about it. There are a lot of acronyms and techie terms that people use to explain it, but essentially it boils down to a very simple concept. It's a method of taking analog audio signals, like the kind you hear when you talk on the phone, and turning them into digital data that can be transmitted over Internet Protocol networks (IP). The basic concept of everything I will be covering in this chapter is that VoIP allows both voice and data communications to be run over a single network, which can significantly reduce infrastructure costs for large and small businesses alike.

To fully understand the way VoIP is revolutionizing the way we communicate and do business, let's engage in a little historical

69

perspective. The traditional phone system that has been around a hundred years is the landline, which is made of copper based wires that physically connect from telephone poles or underground systems to your phones. Obviously the fastest growing aspect of the telecommunications industry over the past decade and a half is the dynamic of wireless/cellular phones. Because of the growth of cell phone use, there has been a huge drop-off in the traditional industry of landlines. Many people are dumping them all together and their main phone numbers are their cell phones.

The market for VoIP started to blossom with the advent of broadband, first with DSL, which allowed phone and cable companies to provide Internet service over cable. As the Internet grew, companies laid down fiber optic networks across the world in an effort to improve the speed and performance of the Internet. Having that faster Internet connection has led to the burgeoning market for transmitting voice communications. The growth of those networks led to the ability to build phone networks using the fiber optic backbone.

The telecommunications companies had the capacity now to add to their services and the major cable companies began to jump in and offer phone service themselves. This, of course, put them on a collision course with traditional phone companies, which continue to work with those old-school copper landlines, also referred to as T1s. A T1 line can carry 24 digitized voice channels, or it can carry data at a rate of 1.544 megabits per second. If the T1 line is being used for telephone conversations, it plugs into the office's phone system. T1s can cost several thousand dollars per month.

ENTER VOIP – AND A LOT OF SAVINGS

Considering that most T1 systems are still based on these expensive copper landlines, it makes sense that VoIP has taken off to the degree it has. The technology has given rise to a new frontier in the telecommunications business, where hundreds of companies—competing like the tech equivalent of the Wild Wild West—are offering VoIP services. These ITSP (Internet telephone service providers) are meeting the needs of companies who are always looking to save money and improve the quality of their customer service. VoIP plays perfectly into this model of saving money while providing these new capabilities. To distinguish old school from new methodology, a clever pejorative acronym was coined: POTS, or plain old telephone service.

In slightly technical terms, the switch involved a move from copper line based phone systems known as PBX—basically a term meaning private branch exchange—to PBX lines that are VoIP. In the past, the phone lines from the phone company plugged into PBX that linked to all the handsets on people's desks. In fact, since 2008, almost 80 percent of all newly installed PBX lines are VoIP. It's hard to fathom the immense quantity of VoIP lines being deployed now, which is dwarfing any remaining demand for copper lines.

Everything is switching now to virtual, software-based PBXs now. What's happening is that VoIP systems are plugging into the same network jacks that computers are plugging into. The new specialized VoIP phones have two jacks built in, one for the network to plug into the wall and another for the PC or Mac to plug into the phone. So that's one of the efficient elements, that the phone – like the computer – is just another device attached to the network. You can plug the phone into the network and don't need a separate phone line. Then you can shop and get your VoIP service from anyone. As this phenomenon keeps growing and becomes the norm, it becomes more reliable, with higher quality and lower costs.

One of the reasons it costs less is that with VoIP you don't have to pay the phone company's excise taxes anymore and just an FCC regulatory and e911 fees. This fee on landlines is added to an excise tax fund that the government draws from to build phone lines in remote places. The government, wanting to ensure that broadband was available to anyone in America, including those in remote areas, has in recent years committed some of this money to build a more extensive broadband system. This has helped to create cottage industries among tech companies serving these rural areas.

UNDERSTANDING THE BOTTOM LINE

Just as the Internet has revolutionized the way we get information and do business, VoIP is helping make our voice communication more efficient. It plays in well to a world gone wireless, allowing businesses and consumers to make fresh new choices they couldn't make even ten years ago. Businesses get lower cost service for their phones and save themselves a lot every month on their phone service, not just because of the aforementioned tax savings but also because the cost of the service is lower. Even outside of the business environment, the use of VoIP makes sense. The change boils down to simple mathematics. If you want two landlines in your home, you have to get two numbers and two sets of copper wires for those lines.

In some areas, the use of copper created a bottleneck situation. I remember a story in Rochester, NY some years ago when the new CEO of Frontier Communications bought a home in an expensive suburb and there were not enough copper lines to have phones in his house. The phone company had to string a whole new cable down the rural road. Now that sounds so primitive. If you have a strong, fast and reliable Internet connection, you can hook up multiple phone lines. For businesses, there is the added upshot of increased Quality of Service (yes, there is an acronym for that – QoS!).

Say you own a small business. Instead of having to have five physical pairs of wires for five phone lines, your Internet connection can send you what they call multiple "sessions," or calls, at one time, so you can have five lines and conversations going at once—without the need for multiple wires. The irony is that we still call these connections "lines," though they are not. It's actually more accurate to say, "You have a call parked on 701," referring to a spot in the system.

INCREASED MOBILITY

The concept of "lines" is so ingrained in our cultural communications psyche that it takes time for people to transition to the concept of having virtual numbers. The amazing part of these numbers is that they can be routed to you from anywhere. With landlines when you called a number, you assumed the person picking up was in a landline at the location tied to the area code and prefix you dialed. Now, a virtual number can be answered in any number of locations, allowing businesses to expand their customer territory.

My IT business is based in Rochester, NY but say I wanted it to have the appearance of having a presence in Syracuse and Buffalo to reach other potential customer and clients throughout New York State. With VoIP, I can have different numbers with appropriate area codes for those other cities. One phone system handles them all, and people from Buffalo don't feel like they are calling someone far away to help them with their business. The same goes with telecommuting. Your employees can be anywhere. We have one employee, who works to help our customers with our VoIP needs, who is based in Florida but most of our customers don't know that. He's got a three-digit extension and customers can place calls to him as if he is in Rochester.

VoIP increases the ability for people to work from home, because the phone in someone's office can be cloned (or "twinned") to the phone in a person's home office. It can be programmed to ring in either or both places. It's fun to imagine being on a working vacation, being at a cottage by the lake or a condo in Florida, yet taking calls from people who have no idea we're not in the office in Rochester. In addition to local number portability, if your company should move to a new physical location, you can keep your numbers and you won't have to do the old school thing with a message on the old line referring callers to the new one.

The simplicity of the connectivity also makes moves in the main office setting easier for your employees. Since plugging in your phone is the same with VoIP as plugging your computer into a network, a simple move into a new office space or cubicle is very easy. In the past, a phone guy had to come out to switch wires so the line would ring in the new space, but now you just plug the phone into the same network jack and you're off and running.

REDUNDANCY

This leads to another important concept known as redundancy. Redundancy as it relates to your VOIP network refers to having alternative routes for your data in the event the main access point fails. If your Internet in one place is down for any reason, the system can be set up to reroute calls to your cell phone or another system. If my network crashed here in Rochester, a client could still call my main number and it could be rerouted to my cell number or to another physical location. This comes in very handy during an emergency, like a natural disaster, when the power is knocked out. If you were a business in the region struck by Super-storm Sandy, for instance, and you had VoIP, you would have been back in business immediately, because rerouting calls this way doesn't depend on working copper-based landlines.

Some people who are used to the old school telecom ways tell me this sounds complicated to them, but I explain it to them in terms of how their cell phone signals work. Your calls go to a tower which is connected with fiber optic cable, and is then transmitted over VoIP to a cell company's switching equipment. So in essence, a cell phone call uses the voice over data technology that VoIP uses. A lot of people get caught up in their fear of new terms and technology, so they don't realize that the calls they already make are being transmitted by VoIP. Understanding that they've been using it without knowing it eases any concerns they have about using the technology on a more extensive level to improve their business' QoS.

IN CASE OF A POWER OUTAGE...

Another understandable point of resistance from old schoolers is being able to use the phones in case of emergency during power outages. The old phone systems had a DC power current supplied by the phone company so that even when the power is out, you can still call 911. This was actually based on an FCC requirement. The phone company had to provide a backup system to the phone network so that even during an outage customers could still pick up a phone and make an emergency call. So how does VoIP duplicate that when its use of cable or DSL is dependent on electricity? Simple – by adding battery backup to VoIP systems.

Batteries are generally included in the VoIP equipment you get from the cable company that will provide power to it so that the phone line doesn't go out when the power goes down. VoIP phones may also come with (here's another great new acronym!) PoE, or Power over Ethernet, in which your network jack can provide power to that phone. On the other end of your network is a PoE switch. Your Ethernet has a larger than normal phone connector feature because only four of its eight internal wires are necessary for an Internet connection. The four unused wires can be used to supply power. More and more users are adding battery power to their Internet connection. Your Ethernet wire can provide power to your phone and the PoE switch can be plugged into your backup battery unit. Ask your VoIP provider to set you up with PoE so that your phone lines are always protected in case of emergency.

FINAL THOUGHTS: FAXES AND BURGLAR/FIRE ALARMS

I wouldn't be surprised if someday soon, 100 percent of new PBX lines going in at private residences and business are VoIP systems. But this leads to a major concern for two important aspects of our lives that have traditionally been tied to copper phone lines: faxing and alarm systems. Many people may simply opt to keep their traditional landlines for their alarm system and fax machines, but some alarm systems now offer cellular connections. So if you want to go exclusively with VoIP, you should contact your alarm company to see about available services. Fax technology is based on traditional phone lines and dial-up modems, but there are new standards for faxing over VoIP. Some manufacturers have multi-functional equipment that includes the T.38 fax relay standard, which was devised in 1998 as a way to permit faxes to be transported across IP networks. Other people are signing up with services that will convert your faxes to pdf files that you can open via email.

Though these technologies are in a transitional phase as the world continues to make its transition to VoIP technology, you can see that the pros of the present and future far outweigh the challenges of adapting from systems we've been used to in the past. If you're not already up to speed with VoIP, I suggest you start investigating the benefits it will provide you in your personal life and in conducting your day-to-day business.

About David

David Wolf is a technology visionary and serial entrepreneur with over 30 years of experience in the IT industry. He enjoys using his technical expertise to help fellow small business owners get the most out of their IT. Whether you have just one PC or large multi-location or multi-server datacenters – David can help you plan and execute the best technology solutions for your business.

His previous experience during the 80's and 90's included positions as founder and President at Vivatron and VivaNET Corporations and he was a Senior Systems Analyst at Unisys, making him both the business and technology expert his loyal clients rely on. David has been a guest speaker on technology at numerous business associations and chamber events.

David is a graduate of the Rochester Institute of Technology and most recently Roberts Wesleyan College with a Master of Science in Strategic Marketing. David has accumulated numerous industry certifications over many years from Microsoft, Cisco, SonicWALL, Allworx, RedHat, SCO Advanced Certified Engineer (ACE) in UNIX and Xenix.

Away from the office, David enjoys spending time with his family and watching his children play ice hockey. His hobbies include scouting, movies, photography and skiing. He also enjoys volunteering his time with Kiwanis International as the Finger Lakes Division Treasurer. David is past member of the board of trustees and VP of Admin and Finance for Temple Sinai in Penfield, NY. David is also a past Chairman of the Board of the Better Business Bureau, Inc., Buffalo, NY as well as served on their board of directors for over 20 years.

You can connect with David at:
davidw@justinc.com
Twitter: @davidawolf
www.superdavewolf.com

CHAPTER 8

THE PERFECT FIT: CHOOSING THE RIGHT LINE OF BUSINESS APPLICATION TO ENHANCE YOUR COMPANY

BY JOANNA SOBRAN AND MICHAEL DUGAN

In seeking the most appropriate line of business applications to enhance their efficiency and productivity, companies generally have two choices. They can look to the market for off-the-shelf packaged solutions or find specialists to help them build custom applications. To the average business owner, this decision of purchasing commercial off-the-shelf (COTS) software or building their own custom application from scratch is a daunting one.

The traditional rule of thumb is that packaged solutions should meet a minimum of 80% of the required functionality for a business. However, most companies choose solutions that have solved only 60% of their operational business needs – leaving them with holes as their business evolves.

While off-the-shelf software is often an attractive choice to business owners for its low initial investment, hidden costs can creep up and surprise you if the product is not a perfect fit for your company. When deciding on which solution will help you grow your business and improve efficiencies, you should consider the requirements of your business from the perspective of business processes, not just from features and functions.

Many times off-the-shelf solutions will meet the functional requirements, but fail to provide a solution consistent with the organization's business processes. When assessing an off-the-shelf solution, there must be a strong consideration on how flexible, extensible and maintainable the application will be throughout the life of the software. Most importantly, you need to ask yourself if the off-the-shelf solution meets your specific business needs. Are you paying for the complexity of many features that aren't necessary for your operations? Keep in mind there is training involved, implementation and maintenance costs, which you should be considering when implementing either solution (off-the-shelf or custom application). Do you have detailed requirements (aka: your "wish list") written out to make the right choice? Do you have the in-house support team to implement either solution?

AN OFF-THE-SHELF PRODUCT SEEMS SO EASY. WHY SHOULD I CONSIDER SOMETHING CUSTOM?

There are certain businesses, those in the healthcare industry for example, where constant changes driven by regulation and mandatory compliance make custom applications a must. Let's imagine a workflow situation in which a healthcare company is still exchanging papers, faxes, and e-mails. A secure electronic custom portal is a much better option that will allow them to meet HIPAA compliance, reduce paper, exchange information quickly and securely, and give them the ability to analyze the data through reports and dashboards.

A business may also consider a custom solution if they have specific goals to meet and they want to be able to modify their applications on an on-going basis, which just isn't possible with most off-the-shelf solutions. Or perhaps they see the value in investing in an application which will provide additional resources and tools to their clients and work to help them grow their business.

Companies often choose to invest in a customized solution as a unique business asset because they have unique operational needs or because they can leverage the technology to differentiate their business from the competition.

Innovation is a key driver to some business owners who want to show, think, feel, and be different from their competitors. Customized digital technology can really give you a cutting edge advantage to stand out from your competitors. While off-the-shelf solutions may seem to be a logical and cost-effective option, since many of the complex features are already designed and developed, other companies in your industry may be using the same thing. Plus the packaged solution may be overkill for what you need.

While there is a lower initial investment in an off-the-shelf solution, a custom application built from scratch specifically for your business may ultimately save you more time and money. Since an off-the-shelf product is a "one-size-fits-all" approach, you may have to invest more time in weeding through all the bells and whistles that you don't need. More time may be spent familiarizing your employees with its features and determining how you can maximize its general features to meet your specific needs.

While there can be a substantial investment in a custom application initially, you will likely find that you will be able to implement it and utilize all its features more easily and in less time. For example, if you involve your staff in its development and essentially convert your manual paper processes to an electronic format, you can create the application with only the features that will directly relate to your business using your company language and operational processes. Your employees will have instant familiarity with the application, it will be more intuitive, and increase their readiness to use it. With a custom application specifically designed for your company, truly the sky is the limit.

If you're not quite ready to build a complete custom application from scratch, there may be hybrid solutions that allow you to take off-the-shelf software and customize portions of the existing framework to make it more aptly meet your needs. There are also custom software interfaces, which can be used to connect various systems with your line-of-business applications, to allow for integration and information sharing between disparate systems.

AN EXAMPLE OF WHY A CUSTOM APPLICATION MIGHT BE THE WAY TO GO.

Not long ago, we were hired by one of the nation's largest health insurance companies to develop a software application that would allow verification of data submitted by medical groups to the payer in order to reduce human error and provide a quick way to view risk scores. By having the capability to view the highest risk scores, medical groups would push to decrease and better align scores with a control group utilized as a benchmark. This would translate into larger financial savings for the insurance company, increased reimbursement for the medical group, and better patient care due to the centralized approach of recording the patient progress.

We were able to perform an analysis and present a solution to the insurance company based on their specific business needs. The combination of healthcare and technology expertise made our tech company the ideal choice to develop the new web-based secure tool that is accessible from anywhere and is independent of the Electronic Health Record (EHR) system of the medical group, providing the opportunity to serve the needs of various groups in a flexible and affordable way. The solution not only provided access to a modern application but also ensured medical groups have a centralized location for document management by housing the document repository and the application on a custom portal.

The improvements were dramatic. Among other key results, users were provided with an easy to use, web-based tool to aid the care management process for the top 10% of the patient population that accounts for over 60% of the costs. Patients began benefiting from a more personalized and comprehensive approach that managed not just a single disease at a time, but the complex relationship between multiple/chronic diseases, lifestyle choices, and untreated conditions. The ROI (Return on Investment) from these features will be substantial since the product is scalable and allows for lower cost modifications.

HOW DO I KNOW WHICH IS BEST FOR ME?

The answer lies in outlining a complete picture of what your business requires from the software. There are some very basic steps you can take to determine your specific needs and how to negotiate the various steps of implementing them.

Get Real.
Identify where you lack efficiencies, where you may be losing money, and anything that is currently keeping you from growing the value of your business. What are your gaps? What is taking you too long to do? If you can't manufacture any more products during a single day, think about how you can get more dollars out of what you do make.

The process of evaluating your strengths and weaknesses is called a Business Process Review. It requires participation from all "business champions" in your organization meaning that the experts in each area – accounting, operations, sales – will be thoroughly interviewed in order to answer the questions of "how do we do it today" and "how can we do it better." It is the opportunity to redesign business processes, change accounting and reporting structure, streamline activities, introduce new capabilities and ultimately revamp the outdated environment and excite employees about the new opportunities.

Create a wish list and an RFP.
Combine your wish list, goals, and philosophies to create a Request For Proposal (RFP) to find a technology partner that will help you implement the right solution for your business. Send this RFP out to technology vendors to determine if they are a good fit to deliver the custom or off-the-shelf application that you need. Include detailed questions which will help you determine the right people to help you accomplish your goals. Ideally, it will be someone who understands your industry very well. Beyond this, question what kind of support they will offer after they have delivered the application to you as you will want someone to help you maintain and grow it. We like to say that the RFP is like a "dating profile" for those looking for the ideal "marriage" with a development company. It's a clever way to emphasize the importance of an optimal ongoing relationship.

Ask yourself, "Do you have the in-house support to manage and grow this technology solution and use it to its fullest potential?"
Sometimes companies make mistakes of thinking that their new software solution is going to magically build and maintain itself, but that's obviously not reality. So you need to consider involving your entire team (or a large portion of it) to determine and define the requirements for the application and what it is going to do for you. It's the tech equivalent of training and investing time and money in an employee. Get your team

on board to develop it and grow it, because they're the ones who will be using it on a daily basis. If you don't embrace it and put it to work, there's no point in having it. Now that you have the application, make sure everyone is integrating it into their daily workflow.

Finally, determine how you can use the software to create value in your business, especially if you're considering growing or selling. This comes back to value via greater efficiency. Use the application to rid yourself of the burden of manual administrative tasks. Keep identifying ways to become more productive. For instance, if you have an organization or department of 50 people and they make an average salary of $50,000 per year, that's $2.5 million. If you remove ten percent of the time they take to do administrative tasks then that means you are saving $250,000 a year in wasted administrative time costs. They no longer need to spend this much time devoted to those tasks because the software solution you have implemented helped you with those things. Your employees can put that extra time into profit making, business growing endeavors like customer service, sales, and marketing. More employee productivity generates dollars, which helps your company grow and thus increase its value should you decide to ever sell it.

I'VE DECIDED I WANT TO DEVELOP MY OWN APPLICATION. WHAT IS THE PROCESS LIKE AND HOW DO I STAY ON TIME AND ON BUDGET?

Let's say you have found a company you want to work with on building your new application software. Before you sign on the dotted line, you'll want to ask the specialists these two important questions:

- What are your processes for development, implementation, and project management?
- How will you work internally with us?

We like to use the term "Agile Methodology" to describe the ideal working situation. That just means flexibility and a willingness to adapt to factors around them. It's important to know what everyone expects of everyone else and what the specific internal necessities are. Remember you are a Stakeholder in this operation and so those you hire should make you part of the requirement-gathering and implementation process. You should work with the specialists you hire on creating a feasible timeline and make sure they can hold to it.

Be sure to choose a company and people you like and one who can communicate with you and who understand you and your needs. If you find an application that intrigues you but its developers are in foreign countries or don't speak your language, your product is going to suffer. Compatibility is key in choosing the right people to help you with your new business applications! Each application development or implementation team will have their own process, and if they're good, they will want to have you involved in the process. They should have a "Stakeholder Review," which allows you to spend time with them during the creation phase to make sure everything is done to your specifications.

SO HOW TO MAKE THE MOST OF MY NEW SOFTWARE AND CONVERT IT TO REVENUE?

By now, you're seeing a pattern in this chapter. Everything goes back to efficiency. Bottom line – you can't run a business without the right applications to support it. Whatever line-of-business application you choose, your new software should allow you to repurpose your staff to eliminate those administrative tasks.

Here's your chance to be innovative. If you have a custom solution that no one else in your market has, it's like your "secret sauce" that allows you to stand out and even, when appropriate, charge more money for your services. If you were just a service provider before, maybe now you can offer technological tools to your customers that help them save time and money in their own business. If you have an off-the-shelf solution, you can improve efficiencies and save time and money.

Creating a portal that allows your customers to go in and download different company templates or other self-sufficient elements will facilitate your interactions, and those offerings add value to your services. You also may not have to spend as much time educating your clients because everything is there in one portal, including educational videos that explain basic aspects of your business to existing and potential clients. This higher level of collaboration helps you stand out in your market. Maybe your application allows you to interact regularly with clients and update them via alerts. You only have to do something once to reach many customers at the same time and securely.

IT'S WORTH MENTIONING AGAIN:

Let's review the basics of what you should do once your business application system is implemented… maintain your product, grow it, keep your wish list growing and let the system allow you to be more efficient. Your digital assets should be treated as a valued employee and cherished and cultivated as such. This "employee" will never quit, show up late, or make mistakes. Keep them growing and investing in them just as you do with those who work for you.

About Joanna and Michael

Joanna Sobran and Michael Dugan launched MXOtech in August of 2005. MXOtech provides IT consulting services with a focus on Custom Software Development and Managed IT Services. Their vision for MXOtech grew from Joanna and Michael's collective experience in the technology and healthcare industries. Their practical business approach combined with their hands-on experience and wide knowledge in the software development and managed IT services field, became the solid foundation to build their own successful business. They share a passion for taking ideas and turning them into applications and solutions that fuel growth. Some of MXO's healthcare applications have been nominated for Innovation Awards and adopted by Fortune 1000 companies to be utilized on an enterprise-wide level.

Joanna is the President and Co-Founder of MXOtech. Joanna is focused on delivering a high-level customer experience with innovation. She is passionate about helping her clients grow their businesses. Whether it's through using better technology solutions, improving operations or education, she treasures her clients and truly cares about their success.

Joanna is the decision maker and steering wheel of MXOtech. She focuses on vision, product development, marketing and strategy. Joanna knows how important the human factor is for the success of a company, therefore she hand picks everyone on her team to bring the best products and services to her clients.

Michael Dugan is the Chief Technology Officer and Co-Founder of MXOtech. Michael's passion lies in bringing his clients' visions to life. His creativity and knack for planning, developing and implementation of value-rich solutions consistently surpass client expectations. Michael serves as the catalyst of business growth and profitability for many of MXOtech's clients.

In his role as Scrum Master, Michael leads the development team and manages all the software and application development projects for MXOtech. He focuses on fostering a holistic approach to product development to reach a common goal and delivering the best possible solutions for his clients.

CHAPTER 9

WHAT IT SHOULD COST

BY FRANK BRAVATA

According to Forrester Research Inc., in most industries, companies should be spending between four and eight percent (4-8%) of gross revenues on Information Technology (IT) costs. **If your company is under-spending on technology, it may be missing out on a competitive advantage that your competition is enjoying.**

Unfortunately, there is a lot of pushback from business owners when it comes to investing in their IT infrastructure because business owners often don't understand the complexities of the technology it takes to run and protect their business. Understandably, the cost for every business will be different because every technology solution will be unique to each business. If a solution costs you, for example, $1,500, how much more productivity will you be able to get out of your employees? How much less risk do you have at that point because your data is being properly backed up and maintained? Smart business owners find that the value gained by the increase in productivity and the prevention of lost data far outweigh the costs of having a business class technology system.

Not every business wants to run their business with the efficiencies and the safety net that can be provided by a proper IT solution. There is a big difference in a company that sees the opportunity to invest in technology and reap the benefits of it, as compared to the business that considers IT to be an unnecessary cost and chooses to pay the bare minimum just to keep their systems running. The latter companies will always lag behind the companies that invest in their IT infrastructure. Their employees will be less productive and they will be constantly dealing with IT-related downtime in their business. They are so focused on spending as little as possible that they don't realize how much it is costing them by not having best-in-class technology service. I have seen it proven over and over again that a company with the proper IT infrastructure will have a competitive advantage and they will capitalize on that advantage.

NOT HAVING BUSINESS CLASS TECHNOLOGY CAN BE COSTLY

Not too long ago I had a discussion with a prospective client who owned a small business, but spent as little money as possible on IT. They didn't even have a business class firewall. They only thing they had protecting their network was a residential quality router that you would have in your home. The owner came to me originally because he said he was having a problem with his Internet provider and was not able to send email. He had an important report that he needed to email but wasn't able to because of his network problems.

When I logged onto his computer, I found there were ten different toolbars that installed themselves. He had contracted a virus and the virus was using his entire network to send out spam. As a result, his network was blacklisted and no one in his entire company was able to send out email. My team and I discovered that only half the computers in his office were equipped with antivirus programs. As we began cleaning up the virus he noticed he was missing some files. He asked if we could help him restore the files from his backup. However, his backup was outdated and even had the original tape still in the drive. No one had ever changed the backup tape! So, there was actually no backup for his more recent data. As a result, he had to go through a process of recreating files and tracking down files in his email archive and other sources. It took him about three weeks to get his data back. It was at that point that he recognized the value in having an appropriate IT infrastructure in place and asked us to set up the proper solution for him.

The first thing we did was install a business-class firewall to keep his network safe and updated his backup system. Then we proceeded to update and add other necessary features until he had a stable infrastructure that would give him the assurance he wouldn't face the same problems down the road. He was also running a custom software package and paying every year for the software and maintenance. Despite paying for the updates, he never applied any of them and was missing out on dozens of new features and stability improvements. We contacted the vendor on his behalf and helped him get his system up to date. After completing all the necessary updates he was amazed at how much more efficiently his business operated.

In this situation, it cost $6,000 just to clean up his network. Then he had the soft costs of his time to search for missing files and data, as well as numerous other related expenses. Unfortunately, this technology crisis cost him close to $20,000. He could have saved himself thousands of dollars and dealt with much less stress if he would have contacted us a few years earlier to help him design and implement the business class solution he needed. Now he pays a flat fee per month and is very glad to send me that check because he now has the assurance that his technology needs are covered especially during this time of strict regulatory compliance in his industry. Fines in his industry can reach as high as $1 million for a data breach.

Unfortunately, this type of scenario is not uncommon. It's very important that business owners understand that there is a definite cost to not having the proper technology in place and monitored.

WHY IS IT SO EXPENSIVE?

Whenever we are asked what it's going to cost to have a technician on site for a non-managed customer, there is usually a "sticker-shock" type response. But they don't think about everything that goes on behind the scenes to enable us to be able to respond quickly to a customer that needs their systems back up and running immediately. We aren't the guy that works out of their car that comes by now and again to remove a virus from one of your computers. Someone like that you can get for $30 or $40 an hour. But if you have a problem three years from now with something we already setup for you, we will know the exact piece of equipment or software application and can probably have the issue resolved for you without having to leave our office. If you try to find the $30 an hour guy after three years it probably will be nearly impossible. By that time he probably will have moved on to another job and will no longer be providing IT services out of his car.

As with any business, every time our phone rings, I have a cost. I have office space expenses, vehicle expense, gas costs, vehicle maintenance, etc. Everything I do has an associated cost. We are always looking for the best technicians and we don't pay a cheap wage to get the best. It only makes sense to pay for the best so we can deliver the best service to our customers. It makes more sense to pay someone a good wage who can get a problem resolved in an hour than to pay someone a lower wage who will take four hours to do the same job. Our customers expect fast service from us because if their technology is not working properly, it is costing them money in lost work productivity from their employees.

We invest a lot of money in our own software so we will be able to respond to our customer's needs in the fastest way possible. For example, the remote maintenance platform we use costs a lot of money, but it saves us as well as our customers a lot of time. It's not just the cost of buying the platform, but we also have thousands of IT hours and resources invested in customizing it to best fit the needs of our customers. With this platform, we can make software updates on hundreds of machines overnight and the customer doesn't have to experience any downtime for their employees. Our customers absolutely love this feature.

We also have a PSA (Professional Services Association) package that we utilize. If one of our customers emails us with a problem, a work order is automatically produced through this system and the proper technicians are automatically notified. This enables us to address the customer's problem in the most time-efficient manner possible. If a technician doesn't respond in the allocated time, a message is automatically generated to escalate the issue to the next level. As a result, we don't have any missed service calls and every customer's issues are handled promptly. Again, this is a platform on which we have spent a lot of money and customization time to better serve our customers. Because of this investment in technology, we can guarantee our highest priority clients a four-hour onsite time guarantee and a fifteen-minute remote response guarantee. Compare that to someone who is a single operator who may not respond until the next day. Depending on your business, a next day response time could range anywhere from a significant inconvenience to it being a real drain on productivity and revenue.

The bottom line is, doing IT the right way costs money. For us, to hire the best technicians and use the best software and tools, it is quite expensive. But, at the end of the day, the results we achieve make it more than worth it for our clients.

WAYS COMPANIES CAN DRIVE DOWN THEIR IT COSTS

• Standardization

Standardization of your equipment and software in your business can go a long way to help you drive down your IT costs. Southwest Airlines is a great example of standardization. They have a single model airplane and all of their techs are trained on the same model. All the parts they order are for the same model. Their entire operation is built around one model of airplane. This model enables them to operate at the highest level of skill and efficiency in this area of their organization.

The same concept holds true for companies and their computer technology. When a company has five computers or more, they are better off to have all the computers be the same model. If all your computers are the same, they can all be configured the same, with the same software, same parts, etc. If one machine has a hard drive crash, you can pull a hard drive out of another machine that isn't being used for a very quick fix.

My IT provider business is based on this same model. I like to use the same equipment in the offices of all my customers because I know the product, I know what works well for specific applications, I know what parts to have on hand, etc. All my techs are experts in that equipment. The vendors that we purchase from are familiar with us because they know we use the same equipment for all our clients. Standardization makes things much easier for us as well as our clients.

• IT Responsiveness – Gotta have it!

It is imperative for your business to have an IT provider that has quick response time. Whenever a business has down time there are definite costs associated: lost revenue, lost employee productivity, lost sales, etc. The reason we operate so efficiently as an IT provider is so we can mitigate the downtime our customers may experience. If we operate efficiently, that means we will be available to help our customers operate at maximum efficiency. Prompt IT provider response time will save you money.

• Be Proactive Not Reactive

Taking proactive steps to prevent a problem will save you much more money than it costs to react to a problem. Establishing a business class technology infrastructure and keeping it maintained will enable your systems to work more efficiently – which translates into a more efficient business. A qualified IT provider will make sure all your equipment and software applications are current and running at optimized levels. Any updates can normally be done remotely and with no downtime for your employees. That's a lot cheaper than having to pay someone to come to your office to update 40 machines and having employees wait outside their cubicle while the tech is updating their software.

• Align IT With Business Goals

Whenever I discuss IT with one of my customers, it is very important for me to understand where their business is going and knowing their short-term and long- term goals. I want to know what's taking place now, what they anticipate in the near future and even in five years. It's important to know this so we don't waste their money on technology that will be useful today but may not be compatible with their plans a year from now. We always try to match the IT solution with the goals of the company. If I know a company is planning to merge with another company in two years, my recommendations may be much different than if they were simply planning to open a new location in a different city in two years.

• Create Efficiencies

I always encourage my customers to centralize, automate, and simplify their technology to help them save money. For example, many times I will go into an office and find ten different versions of an antivirus product and it's not centralized. I recommend they put a business class antivirus on all their machines as well as on the server. Then we can log into their server and see the status on all their machines instead of walking around to each of the machines and opening up the logs to make sure they don't have any viruses waiting to be removed. This can be done with many technology pieces within a business. By centralizing and automating, things are simplified and money is saved.

- **Tax Benefits**

  Discuss with your accountant the tax advantages of utilizing the Hardware As A Service (HAAS) concept for your business. Here's how HAAS works. Let's say your business has ten computers that need to be replaced. Many IT providers will supply the computers and allow you to roll the cost into your monthly agreement. This saves the business the initial capital expenditure of buying ten computers and the associated software. But, there may also be a tax advantage. In this scenario, the new computers are an operating expense and not a capital expense. This means you don't have to go through the depreciation process on the business tax return. Many companies really like this concept for its convenience as well as the tax advantages and it works out especially well with new startups.

THE HIDDEN COST OF CHEAPER SHOPS

While there is often temptation to use a company that is cheaper, or to hire a college student or out-of-work IT professional, these solutions typically wind up costing more in the long run. If someone is working out of their house and they are the cause of a data loss for your company, what will you do? Will you sue the tech? Even if you win the lawsuit, you probably won't ever be able to collect any damages because the tech probably doesn't have any assets. On the other hand, a professional IT provider will carry errors and omissions insurance in case of a lawsuit. Hiring a professional allows you the peace of mind of knowing that their reputation (and business insurance) is on the line.

Many people hire cheap labor without considering the quality of the labor they are hiring. In today's IT world, there is too much technology for one person to be able to grasp and stay up to date on continuously. Whereas, when you have a team of professionals there is a broader knowledge base to be able to handle virtually any IT related issue. In our office, we even have an escalation company we work with in case we ever run into a specialized situation where we need more expertise.

We often are called in to clean up projects that have gone bad or over budget. We often find that these projects were implemented by those lacking the experience or knowhow. Cleaning up a failed project is exponentially more expensive than just getting the job done right the first time. There is just too much risk associated with entrusting your IT needs to those that lack the necessary expertise.

HIRING YOUR IT PROVIDER

With the improved efficiencies of properly installed and maintained technology, IT should pay for itself. Unfortunately, many people consider IT a cost and not an investment, and that simply is not the case. If your IT is working properly, allowing your employees to work at their maximum efficiency, you should be making so much money in your business at that point that the cost for IT will be a very small part of your overall budget.

IT costs vary greatly depending on where you are located. In many major metropolitan areas, an all-inclusive technology package typically will cost between $125.00 to $175.00 per employee per month. In smaller rural areas, you may find this cost to be somewhat less.

I recommend looking for a solution provider that will build a technology stack customized for your company. It will include all of the needed services that your company requires to both survive and to thrive. Things like email, help desk, network security, cloud services, onsite support, mobile device management, backups and disaster recovery, technology consulting, automated maintenance, and training are essential for success in today's business environment. If you aren't taking a proactive approach to these needs, you are putting your company at risk.

About Frank

Frank Bravata specializes in assisting his clients to achieve maximum productivity and profitability from their technology investments. This is accomplished by eliminating frustrating technology headaches, and continuously researching, designing, and implementing the best technology solutions available.

Being interested in computers and electronics from a young age, Frank naturally gravitated to the technology industry. Frank began his professional career in the US Army, training at Fort Gordon, GA (the home of the Army's Signal Corps – the largest communications/electronics facility in the free world). Upon graduation from training and earning the designation of Signal Support Specialist, Frank spent the next 6 years working for the 78th Division of the US Army, helping to oversee the IT infrastructure of the entire Division.

Upon the completion of his military contract, Frank then took his skills to the private sector, working as an outsourced IT consultant for such notable companies as the Partnership for a Drug Free America in New York City and Panasonic USA in Torrance, California. It was working at these companies, as well as at hundreds of other small and medium-sized businesses on the West and East coasts, that Frank began to notice a particularly disturbing trend. Often called in to clean up other company's' failed and stalled projects, Frank realized that far too many technology firms lacked the centralized standards that Frank had grown accustomed to in the military. These projects were often done on a whim with a noticeable lack of oversight and planning, leaving many businesses with blown budgets and less than optimal results. After working under these conditions for almost 4 years, Frank decided to make a change.

In early 2009, Frank started New Millennium Technology Services, a managed-services provider located on Long Island, New York. The goal was simple: to provide local businesses unparalleled technology support while drawing upon his military experience to assist his clients in bringing military-like discipline to their IT projects and procedures. The result has been nothing short of spectacular. His clients enjoy systems that are agile and protected, allowing their businesses to excel in their particular industries.

In early 2012, New Millennium was the recipient of a Business Achievement award by the HIA (one of the largest regional trade associations in the country). That same year, CompTIA (the Computer Trade Industry Association) named New Millennium Technology Services as the first Long Island-based recipient of the Managed Services Provider Trustmark. This certification is awarded to those companies that demonstrate a strict adherence to the managed services model as well as industry best practices in the areas of customer service, documentation, and data safety.

You can connect with Frank at:
Frank@longislandcomputercare.com
www.twitter.com/frankbravata
www.linkedin.com/in/frankbravata
www.facebooks.com/frankbravata

CHAPTER 10

DATA SECURITY:
YOUR BUSINESS' MOST VALUED ASSET - OFTEN IGNORED OR OVERLOOKED

BY KEVIN BOWLING

THE BASICS OF DATA SECURITY

The first questions I ask clients interested in Data Security are basic but crucial: Do you lock the doors of your house at night or when you leave? Do you lock your business doors when you're gone for the day? Then why would you NOT lock your most valued business asset – your data, your files and your network?

Simply stated, Data Security is the practice of keeping data from corruption and unauthorized access, and protecting it from outside destructive forces and the unwanted actions of unauthorized users. The focus behind data security is to ensure privacy while protecting personal or corporate data. So, what are we talking about when we ask, "Is your data secured?" Where are the problem areas?

They are in things that you are no doubt familiar with if you've been Internet savvy for a while – Spam, Antivirus, Spyware, Adware, Malware, Phishing, Network, Operating Systems. Other terms that are part of the Data Security realm that you should already know are "data encryption," "wireless security," email, software, backup, fraud,

97

Internet, Cloud, Social Media, Mobile apps and BYOD, or the practice of "Bring Your Own Device" (allowing employees to work with your business data and information using their own portable devices).

Data Security is no longer limited to PCs and laptops. It is not just about virus protection and firewalls. You have to look at the entire organization and how your network is being accessed. Mobile devices such as smartphones, tablets, remote users with home device; VPNs, and cloud; working from multiple devices and often BYOD require additional security measures. These devices are frequently used to access and store both personal and business information. Mobile devices are more susceptible than desktop systems to loss and theft. You can reduce the risk of someone accessing personal and business data when your mobile device is lost or stolen by applying safeguards to the device such as a program to wipe all data stored on the device or having policies in place for employees to report any device lost, stolen or compromised.

WHY IT'S MORE IMPORTANT NOW THAN EVER BEFORE

This past year, the U.S. government adapted a final rule to allow for the enforcement of The Health Insurance Portability and Accountability Act of 1996 (HIPAA), which includes federal protections for individually identifiable health information and various related patients rights. The law exists to protect Social Security numbers and to prevent identity theft, to enact penalties on those who steal people's medical records. In light of the government finally having the power to crack down on violations – with stiff fines and penalties for data being lost and/ or inadvertently sent to the wrong people – tight data security is more important than ever. One company in Tennessee was fined $25,000 per record that was lost. As these protective laws change in the medical records realm, there will be even more regulations in the future.

I've heard terrible stories about theft from emails inadvertently sent to the wrong people. Customers sent sensitive patient information to the wrong doctor, who started calling all those patients to try to steal business away from a competitor. Data theft and leakage is not just an issue with medical records but also of course with customers' credit card information. If a company has that data stored in systems that are then compromised, it's an open door to mass identity theft and fraudulent credit card purchases. You hear about this happening in retail stores, but it also happens at higher levels when hackers tap into a supposedly secure network and access the electronically-stored information.

As technology has evolved, the "industry" of professional hacking (part of a massive wave of Cybercrimes) has grown tremendously. I've been at security conferences where they show pictures of buildings in China filled with nothing but hackers trying to find security holes to access information in the U.S. This is done not only to gain information from military organizations – which could cause major national security risks – but also finding ways into networks to steal information about corporations and individuals.

While the buildings in China are powerful illustrations of the massive problem, we have plenty of skilled big bad cyberwolves in the U.S. as well. Here are just a few sobering statistics:

1. The 2009 Open Security Foundation report claimed that 30% of security violations come from *inside* the organization, and

2. Trend Micro reports that 81% of organizations have suffered at least one data breach over the past two years.

TAKING A LAYERED APPROACH TO SECURITY

So what can you as a private individual or business owner do to protect your data from being victimized?

One of the most important things is using what is called a "layered approach" and not relying on just one form of data security. The more layers you put between you and those trying to get in, the better.

These are the **Top Five** areas at a minimum to have security:

- Firewall
- Antivirus/Antispyware
- Secured Wi-Fi
- Social Engineering – train users not to share
- Email Encryption/Spam Filtering

If someone wants to get at the information on the computer, they have to get through the firewall first, then they have to log on so they need your password. And if they're trying to install spyware, then you of course, must have a strong Antivirus program too. It's about having multiple layers to get one thing accomplished. It seems like a lot of work, but if your data is protected, it's worth every ounce of effort.

KEY PROBLEMS AND EFFECTIVE SOLUTIONS

Scammers, hackers and identity thieves are looking to steal your business information. There are steps you can take to protect yourself such as security software that updates automatically, protect your passwords and use a mix of letters, numbers, special characters and at least 10 characters. Use encrypted websites (https) for security, and don't assume Wi-Fi hotspots are secure.

Encryption scrambles the information you send over the Internet into a code. Encryption is the most effective way to secure your network from intruders. If you have older routers consider buying a new router with WPA2 to protect against most hackers. Wireless routers come with encryption feature but it must be turned on. Wireless Networks connect through "access points" or other wireless devices like a cable modem or wireless router. Any computer with a wireless card can pull the signal from the air and access the Internet if not properly secured. This might not seem like a big deal, but if they can connect to your wireless network this might inadvertently give them access to your local network as well, and anything data within it.

Here's another problem. Have you ever opened an email or text to see a message like…"We suspect your account for unauthorized transactions." Or, "Our records indicate that your account was overcharged." Then there was the one this year from BBB that your business was reported for negative activity.

These are all examples of Phishing, which is the act of attempting to acquire information by masquerading as a trustworthy entity in an electronic communication. Communications purporting to be from popular social web sites, auction sites, banks, online payment processors or IT administrators are commonly used to lure unsuspecting public. They're all ways for hackers to try to get your business or personal information such as credit cards, bank account numbers, passwords, etc. Legitimate companies do not ask for this information via email or text. Never reply or click on the links in these types of messages.

Phishing emails may contain links to websites that are infected with malware, viruses and spyware, which are then installed on your computer or mobile device without your consent. They will cause your device to crash or allow criminals to monitor and control your online activity to steal personal information, send spam and commit fraud. At a minimum, have anti-virus and anti-spam software and a firewall and set these to update automatically. Do not click on links or open attachments in emails unless you trust the source. Only download and install software from websites you trust. Also be warned: free games or free software can come with malware. Make sure your browser setting is on "medium" at minimum and use the pop-up blocker. A few signs that you have malware on your computer include: your computer slowing down, crashes, won't shut down, displays web pages you didn't intend to visit or sends emails you didn't write.

The most common online scams these days include: work-at-home scams, weight loss claims, lotteries scams, miracle cures, debit relief scams, online dating scams and even tech support scams. Examples you may remember of password breaches from hackers include:

- 6.5 million LinkedIn passwords posted and 60% were hacked within days.
- eHarmony reported 1.5 million of its passwords were uploaded following the same attachment that hit LinkedIn.
- Yahoo Voices admitted that nearly 500,000 of its own emails and passwords had been stolen.
- In addition, U.S. Senator Joseph Lieberman pointed to massive recent attacks targeting Bank of America, JPMorgan Chase, Wells Fargo, Citigroup and PNC Bank.

At the end of the day, do not forget to train your staff. My motto has long been, *The security of your data is only going to be as strong as the individuals using the systems.*

SECURITY ISSUES WITH BYOD

Technology has made sure we never ever have to be disconnected from our jobs. But BYOD is a security risk for companies. A recent Harris Interactive Poll found that than 50 percent of employees currently use portable devices, which take sensitive information outside the company walls. Now those portable devices include not only smartphones and tablets, but also laptops and flash drives. The vast majority of companies allow employees to use those devices and have an encryption policy for those devices, the poll found, but only 34 percent actually enforce those policies on personal devices (and just 35 percent for company-owned devices).

One way to secure BYOD is require devices to be configured with passwords, prohibit specific types of applications from being installed on the device or require all data on the device to be encrypted. There are also numerous "Social Security Threats" (i.e. Social Network issues), including data that can seep out, be accessed by or otherwise compromised via connections to the Internet, Facebook, Twitter, LinkedIn, Instagram, Flicker and basically any social networking sites.

EXAMPLES OF REAL LIFE INCIDENTS

One of my customers was experiencing multiple attempts on their network from hackers and it was literally happening multiple times a week. The hackers' attempts were blocked due to having a firewall in place. The firewall sent out notifications to us when the attempts were made. Through monitoring the network activity we had a proactive solution in place therefore allowing the customers network data to stay secure.

A business email was hacked due to not using strong passwords. For example, their last name was the password. A hacker was able to get into their email server and was able to start spamming, which placed them on multiple blacklists that took weeks to resolve and made them lose productivity due to not being able to send emails to their customers.

Typical examples we see regularly when doing Business Network Assessments are:

1. Old user accounts still active for past employees.
2. Security updates not being applied to computers, servers and network equipment.
3. Servers with confidential information being accessed from the Internet without security.
4. Wireless networks being wide open and connected to confidential data.

PREPARING FOR THE FUTURE

So what can your company do to protect your data and prepare for 2014? Here is a list of basic considerations:

- Size does not matter, attackers target everyone, remain vigilant on protecting your devices, your networks and your data.

- Securing sensitive or confidential data, implement security guidelines such as strong passwords, and caution using the web and downloading applications.

- Inventory all files, equipment and know where your business stores important information.

- Backup plan in case of service disruption, corrupted data, stolen data, natural disaster or contingency for business as usual.

- Security on mobile devices, protecting from malware and other threats. Add the feature to erase data when the device has been lost or stolen.

- Protect your business against attackers; virus, spam and malware. Make sure security patches are applied to network equipment, servers, workstations, laptops or any other device accessing the network.

- Making sure security patches are applied to your equipment. This not only refers to your workstations and servers but also mobile devices and more importantly network equipment.

- Use Spam filters and Firewall updates.

- Monitoring hardware, disk space, servers, workstations, error logs and alerts.

- Keep your server room, cabling and equipment properly set up and physically safe.

- Training your employees on security is your first line of defense and having a clear password policy.

IN CONCLUSION

As an IT professional for the past 27 years, I realize that my greatest satisfaction is helping my clients secure their systems and data, knowing that we have helped them get and stay protected – which in turn assures that they will stay in business, avoid fines and potential lawsuits related to data loss and be able to assure their own customers and clients that they are in good, safe hands. You can't put a price on peace of mind, which is the end result of their knowing that they are safe. It's our job to worry about their data security so they can put their focus where it should be – on their business. If, heaven forbid, something dramatic happens, we make sure they're able to continue working.

It wasn't that long ago that everyone feared Technology, but today we cannot manage without Technology. What are the risks of today in Business? ...the loss of customers, revenue, and productivity and possibly your business?

Knowledge of today's risk in data security is the key to a successful business.

About Kevin

Kevin Bowling started his fascination with computers at twelve years of age taking apart and putting computers together. Kevin attended college to learn the computer and network industry. This began his career at Intergraph as a Technician, and worked his way up to a System Engineer. Kevin became a Field Engineer for Intergraph covering the lower Southeastern United States.

As a natural progression, he shifted his focus into security along with getting certifications with Microsoft MCSE Security, Cisco CCNA, Linux LPIC-2, Sun Solaris SCSA, and CompTIA Security+ among others. After gaining the work experience, Kevin then moved into training as a Microsoft Certified Trainer at Virginia College – providing training for upcoming engineers.

Kevin Bowling is the owner of Integration, a fast growing and ever-changing IT Company focused on Security and Managed Services. Kevin, who has a Bachelor's degree in Management Information Systems, has over 25 years' experience in the IT industry.

Kevin started Integration when he saw the need for IT Consulting and Managing networks for Small to Medium Business. Kevin's true passion is going into companies, finding and helping to prevent problems. Whether it's your current IT or your company, Kevin just wants to make sure your business has the most up-to-date proactive solutions needed to keep your business successful in today's constantly-changing technology realm.

CHAPTER 11

BRANCH OFFICE AND REMOTE WORKERS

BY JOHN RUTKOWSKI

HOOK US UP!

The phone rings, it's one of my best clients, an architect that has just won a huge project. He says: "We need more space for people; we just got a great deal on space just down the street. Hook us up and make it happen! People are moving in next week. Bye."

Whoa! I call back, get the address and start my research on what data circuits are available at that location. It turns out his new office was in a technology desert. There were no affordable data circuits to connect his branch office. So rather than spending a normal $125 to $200 per month, he had to spend $700 a month on a circuit that was barely usable. His good deal on space was because no one had any Internet service at that location and no one wanted to rent the space without Internet.

Lesson Learned: Before signing any leases on new office space, check with your technology consultant to see what kinds of data connections are available to you. Factor in those prices as part of the cost of your space and overhead.

THINK SPEED!

As your business begins to grow, you will outgrow your office space or you may have a project that needs staff closer to the project site. So how do your grow from one office to a series of branch offices?

Let's think **speed**. Your current network of PCs communicates on a **gigabit Ethernet** network that is transferring data at 1,000,000,000 bits per second. (And if you have not replaced your network switch in the last 5 years, you might be running 10 (100 Mbps) or 100 times slower at 10 Mbps.) The traditional DSL or T1 data circuits run at 1.5 Mbps. That's a thousand times slower than your network connection. Think about it, can you run your business 1,000 times slower than you operate today?

Think about filling a swimming pool with a straw vs. a fire hose. They both will do the job, but the smaller connection takes a lot longer for it to fill the pool. Same for data circuits.

The average cable modem connection is 20 Mbps download by 5 Mbps upload. **BEWARE**: the circuit providers are always advertising download speed, but a business typically sends as much data as it gets. So your slowest speed may be the bottleneck in the system.

In my marketplace (metro Philadelphia, PA) the Verizon FIOS (Fiber Optic Service) offers the best for business since the speeds are more symmetrical (same speed up and down) and you can easily increase the speed with a phone call. The general rule is that a fiber data circuit gives better speed and greater reliability, followed by Metro Ethernet, cable, DSL and T1.

You can bond a number of separate circuits together for more speed, and you may want two circuits from different providers. More on that later.

Lesson Learned: Think **speed** before buying the cheapest data connection, your Technology Consultant will look at your business, how you edit and update files, your email load and web browsing, then suggest the proper circuits for you.

FOLLOW THE FLOW

In the old days when the Internet was a safer place, you might have placed a public Internet address on your server so the branch office could access files or databases. NOT ANYMORE! The bad guys are out there looking for systems to attack, they are not looking for your company, they are looking for systems that are not up to date and have security issues that they can attack. (Then they will look at your banking, customer information and your products for information they can sell.) So you need to protect your office by connecting via a Virtual Private Network (VPN) that encrypts and allows connections only to known Internet addresses.

This VPN is provided by a firewall. There are many vendors out there, but you want one that handles the speed of the Internet connection, can bond circuits or provide failover, and does the web filtering and virus protection. This is NOT the router that the Internet Service Provider gives you with your circuit. Your Technology Consultant will weigh all of the factors and make a decision for you. It is something that is maintained daily for virus updates and at least monthly for new features.

Now a VPN must have two different networks to which to connect. This means that both the main office and the branch can't have the same private IP address such as 192.168.1.1 or 10.0.0.0. If your office network is on one of the common default networks, CHANGE IT NOW! You will save yourself a lot of grief and money by picking a unique private address. Sure you can extend your network via a traditional AT&T point-to-point circuit but you'll spend a LOT more money.

Lesson Learned: Have the right firewall and plan your networks BEFORE adding the branches.

WHERE ARE THE FILES?

Now you have two offices connected. Where are you going to store your files? Remember in Lesson 2, its speed, so if you have a lot of files, you need them close to the users. This is the time to talk about the Cloud.

With Cloud computing, your people can work from anywhere, any place, any device. They just need a connection to the Internet. (This brings us to the two data circuits mentioned earlier.) With the Cloud, you run the programs from the cloud so your Internet speed needs are less; you are passing only screen images and keystrokes. If your programs can be installed directly on a server, then you can run the same applications from the Cloud. If you have specialized line of business programs, you may need a dedicated Cloud server.

The Pros and Cons of the Cloud are discussed in another chapter, but it does give you great flexibility, and once on the cloud you can grow or shrink your business without having to buy a lot of equipment up front.

If you decide against the Cloud, then you need to consider having a server in the branch location. This lets them work even if the connection to the main office is down. Microsoft offers a feature called Distributed File System (DFS) that allows you to automatically copy files between office servers. It updates the other branch locations when there are changes to a file.

Having files replicate between branch offices does not negate the need for backup. Because if the files are deleted in one location the deletion spreads to the branch offices. But you can structure your backups so the branch office can be your offsite backup and disaster recovery site, if it's nearby for other workers to use. All branch offices should still be backed up and then the backups replicated to the main office. (This is not tape backup! You backup live during the day to a set of hard disks which replicate to your offsite backup location.)

If you are running your own email servers in-house rather than the Cloud, a central mail server is fine until you have 20 or more at the branch office location, then you should consider an email server there or move all email to the Cloud. But with email being such an important part of business these days, a continuity service that archives your email and allows you to send and receive email even if your server is down should be considered. This gives you instant recovery if there is a problem with your email server or a Cloud mail service.

If your users move from office to office, your login needs to be smart enough to give them the local files, not the one back at the main office. (Remember the Speed Lesson; you don't want people opening files 1,000 times slower than they could.)

Line of business applications that are database driven may need other tools to replicate to a branch. If such replication is not supported, you may be able to host your own private Cloud. The Microsoft Remote Desktop Services (formerly known as Terminal Server) can let the user run programs from the main office via a dedicated server. The program shows as an icon on their desktop, but all of the files and changes stay at the main office. Again make sure the Internet is available, otherwise they can't work.

Lesson Learned: Know how the files will be shared between the branch offices. Use the branch as an offsite backup of data. Replicate data or use a private Cloud to run programs from the main office.

Your computer professional can go through this process with you and create a Roadmap to take you where you want to go.

TALK TO ME!

At your office, it's easy to pick up a phone, dial an extension and talk to a co-worker. But how old is your phone system? Can you add a branch office so everyone is a direct extension and phone calls can be transferred to any person at any office?

Modern phone systems are based on Voice Over IP (VOIP) to make location irrelevant. An extension can be the next desk or around the world. You use your Internet circuits to carry the voice conversations rather than the copper wire provided by the phone company which charges you by distance and per minute for phone calls.

Most VOIP systems offer unlimited calling so your phone costs can drop.

To make the VOIP work smoothly, use the "Follow the Flow" lesson and have the right firewall in place that can give you the best phone service over your Internet connection. It can give the voice calls priority over your Facebook postings.

While you may have some phone equipment in the closet (and that tangle of wires) it gets replaced with a small network switch. The phone is actually a small computer. Anywhere you plug in the phone to the Internet, your calls follow you. You can move to an office, work from home and you are still able to get and place calls just as if you were in the office.

And you will save money! The typical monthly fee for phone service and the new phone equipment is a flat rate that is less than what you are spending today. Most firms save hundreds per month. And you have a simple fixed cost for adding or removing an employee.

Lesson Learned: Move to a modern VOIP phone system, you save money and have greater flexibility. It will pay for itself almost immediately!

REMOTE WORKERS

People working from home or always on the road can either be your most productive employees or your biggest headache. In all of the lessons learned about a branch office, they also apply to that single worker. Remote works still need goals, guidelines, schedules and the ability to stay in touch with the other workers and their managers.

They need a good Internet connection and a secure means of working. It is better for a remote worker to be working in the Cloud or to a hosted business application. You DON'T want them working just on their notebook and keeping all of their files there. If your firm is subject to HIPAA, Sarbanes–Oxley or PCI regulations, you cannot afford to have an employee keeping files on their laptop. If it gets lost or stolen you don't want to deal with the regulatory nightmare, possible fines and costs of corrective actions.

Notebook users are the greatest threat to company security. You don't know where they have been and what viruses they may have acquired while using unprotected Internet connections.

You never want remote workers having a direct Virtual Private Network (VPN) connect back to your servers and office network. If they get infected when working remotely, it can spread to your office.

A Secure Sockets Layer (SSL) VPN connection to programs is acceptable. Only keystrokes and screen images are exchanged. The SSL VPN can also setup a tunnel for all Internet traffic to go through your office firewall to protect the user and to keep people from "sniffing" the traffic when they are using the free Wifi at the coffee shop.

All mobile devices be it notebook, laptop, tablet or mobile phone that connects to company resources should have the following:

- Agent to update the software and track location.
- All devices need a PIN, swipe pattern, fingerprint or password to access.
- The ability to wipe the data off the device remotely if it's lost or stolen. (And people need to be trained to report it BEFORE they get a replacement.)
- Antivirus software.
- Minimal rights on the computer so they can't install software (or viruses).
- A Human Resources Policy stating that it is prohibited from keeping company data on personal devices. This means if you want them to have email on a cell phone, you provide the phone so you can control the data.

The "Bring Your Own Device" (BYOD) is seen as a cost saving, but you lose control over security and company data. So consider the cost of a hack, leak or malicious use of data. It could cost you a lot more than the cost of those devices. Your provide, you control.

Lesson Learned: Remote Workers need the proper resources to protect the company and keep the remote workers productive.

So have fun, grow your business, open new locations. To prosper, follow the lessons learned:

1. Know the Internet speed and costs before signing a lease or buying a new office location.

2. Speed! Electronic documents have weight and size. Buy the fire hose, not the straw.

3. Your firewall is the most critical piece of equipment to keep you safe and online.

4. Know your files, have a sharing strategy and backup plan.

5. You have got to communicate. A modern phone system gives you that and reduces costs.

6. Remote workers need love and protection. Keep them safe and productive.

I have been networking businesses for over 27 years. These lessons learned are in place daily at my client's locations, working every day to keep them productive. Philadelphia, Wilmington, New York, Chicago, Washington, Atlantic City, Las Vegas, Dallas, San Francisco, San Diego and China are all connected, working together and talking to one another – from 5 person firms to over 150 employees per business.

About John

John Rutkowski has successfully launched, operated and managed four businesses so far in his business career. While the types of businesses might seem unrelated, they have all dealt with building solutions for a client's problems.

He has the knack for seeing the flaw in a pile of perfection. But then again, it's not perfect.

His education started with a lot of family travel. While he never moved from the family home, he had visited most of the lower 48 states before high school. "Travel exposes you to new ideas, culture and thinking."

At the University of Virginia he studied Architecture, following in the family business, but ended up with a BS in Commerce. "I was the long-haired hippy in the business school." But that led him to be the first in his class to have a job offer before graduation.

John founded BOLDER Designs in 1986 with the then new solution of CAD software for Architects and Engineers. Being that such clients need to collaborate, he built up his business around the networking of such clients and provided solutions to their growing Branch Office and Remote Worker needs. Hence this chapter in the book.

It is said that you become the people you hang out with, John is proud to be a contributor along with the other authors of this book. He has grown through their contributions to the book and looks forward to writing another one with them.

John has spoken nationally at numerous technology events, giving keynotes on how to transform and grow your business.

You can connect with John at:
me@JohnRutkowski.com
www.linkedin.com/in/johnrutkowski
https://www.facebook.com/BolderDesigns

CHAPTER 12

PROTECT YOUR BUSINESS AND SAVE MONEY WITH VIRTUALIZATION

BY JOHN BIGLIN

In today's tech-driven business era, almost every large company has implemented some form of *Virtualization* within their IT environment as a mechanism to save money, reduce or eliminate downtime and experience many other benefits. Real ROI (Return on Investment) has occurred for many of these firms and most of the benefits of Virtualization can also be experienced by small and medium-sized businesses.

To the typical business owner who may not be super-technical, Virtualization may sound like a vague title for something that they find difficult to understand. Some business owners believe virtualization means that everything becomes "virtual" and "not real" and that it seems very risky to them. It is not as risky as they may think.

Virtualization, although a complex technology, is something that can easily be implemented to help a company protect their data while also save money in the long run. In this chapter, I am going to explain some basic concepts and many of the benefits that you, as a business owner, can experience. My goal is to help you understand why I consider Virtualization a "sleep-aid" for business owners. I feel this way because I have seen how it helps lower some of the worry businesses have regarding the stability, reliability, and security of their IT systems. Also, as a bonus, there is money to be saved, which is always a good thing for any business.

SO WHAT IS IT?

Virtualization, in computing, refers to the act of creating a virtual (rather than an actual, or physical) version of something. This may include, but not be limited to, a virtual computer hardware platform, operating system (OS), storage device, computer network resource or even applications and data. Many people don't realize that the term traces its roots to 1960s mainframes, during which it was a method of logically dividing the mainframes' resources for different applications. It is a concept that takes what is normally a physical IT item, such as a Server or PC, and converts it into data. Think of your PC with all of its contents (operating system, applications, etc.) being combined into a single "snapshot" file, but without the actual physical PC.

Let's use Server Virtualization as an example. Most people are familiar with the concept of a server. That is often times the central computer in a computer room, or data center, that all the computers in the office connect to for functions such as sharing files, printing to network printers, and accessing central applications. We've all felt the pain when a File Server fails because of an unforeseen problem. In most cases, it doesn't matter to the business users what is broken - they just want to know when it will be back up and running. While servers are important, they can become the Achilles heel of the whole office network. Also, if the office experiences a major loss of the server through a fire, natural disaster or theft, the chances of recovering from backup tapes, if they are available, to a different type of server in a different location, are limited.

With Server Virtualization your physical server is essentially converted into a data file(s) that contains all of the attributes of that server including the application data, hardware details, storage, settings, etc. Think of it as a snapshot photo of your server that includes every tiny detail of what is in your server. Once a server is virtualized, it also becomes portable in the sense that it can be backed up, copied, and synchronized to another location in similar fashion as any other data on your network. You still need a physical server to run it, but rather than having to purchase one physical server for each application, you can simply run multiple virtual servers on one physical server, which becomes known as a "Host."

You can also group multiple physical Hosts into what is known as a *Resource Pool* that acts as one big Host group. A piece of software called a Hypervisor runs on the Host, instead of a traditional Windows operating system. The Hypervisor manages how the virtual servers use the physical resources of the hosts. See the diagram below for more info:

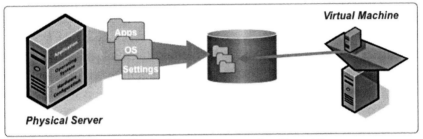

Figure 1. Physical Server converted to Virtual Server

SAVING REAL MONEY, NOT VIRTUAL MONEY

Once your servers are virtualized, the next time you need another server, you typically would not need to purchase a whole new server. Instead, you can dynamically create another virtual server in your resource pool – which saves both time and money. Software licenses must still be purchased, but you don't have to waste time procuring a physical server each time you need one. Most people think the savings simply comes from not having to invest in new hardware, but there's a less obvious area of savings: power and cooling costs. Servers consume a lot of energy and create a ton of heat. By employing the use of virtual servers, instead of physical servers, money will be saved on basic electricity costs and perhaps air conditioning costs as well. Even more savings can occur when a firm looks to set up a disaster recovery center because fewer, and in some cases less powerful, servers and storage components can be used instead of procuring an identical copy of every production server.

FAULT TOLERANCE: REDUCED OR ELIMINATED DOWNTIME

Years ago, it was a "best practice" to run one application on an individual server. As an example, the common thinking was that businesses would not want their Billing System to be impacted if their e-mail system was bogging-down that same server's resources. Likewise, in a shared server setup, if any scheduled maintenance occurred on one system, requiring a reboot, it would bring down any other system running on that same server. Therefore, separate servers were purchased for each business application.

Over the years however, as PCs evolved into much faster systems, file servers evolved into machines with blistering speed and so much capacity that they would typically run at only 5% average processing power, or utilization. Five Percent! That sure seemed like a waste of computing horsepower and money. Eventually, scientists and engineers came up with a way to virtualize servers so that they were isolated when running in a hypervisor. This way, if one was to crash, it wouldn't affect any of the other virtual servers running within that same resource pool. Remember, a resource pool is essentially a group of physical server hosts that operate as one collective group to host and manage virtual servers. In many cases you could run a 10-to-1 ratio of virtual servers to physical hosts, thereby saving money on hardware, power, cooling as well as other costs.

Since the Resource Pool can dynamically manage the Virtual Servers as needed, a hardware failure typically does not stop the servers from running completely. For example, if a video card or other component fails on one of the servers in a resource pool, the Hypervisor can automatically move virtual servers into non-affected areas of the resource pool. A technician can replace hardware components from the failed host computer without the end-users even noticing because the other host(s) are running the servers virtually. That means that the risk of server downtime is dramatically reduced, or even eliminated in many cases.

This may sound somewhat complex, but once it is designed and implemented properly, your business will immediately see the benefits.

DISASTER RECOVERY

Let's start this section with defining what "Disaster" actually means in this context: a total loss of access to a business' IT systems, infrastructure, networks, applications and data for an extended period of time. Years ago, in order to be able to recover IT systems in the event of a disaster, companies had to build identical systems in a separate recovery center– be it a branch office, Business Continuity Service Provider, or some other location. This meant at least duplicating all hardware purchases, and in some cases software purchases, as well as significant expense to replicate system configuration and data so it could be usable at the recovery site.

Traditionally, firms would spend tens of thousands of dollars developing a Disaster Recovery Plan, which typically was a set of big binders full of chapters and pages that (hopefully) provided detailed instructions for firing up the Recovery Site, preparing it for production use, and loading the latest applications and data onto it. Most of the time, these plans simply did not work.

Were they horrible plans? Not necessarily. Were they missing key information? Sometimes. But most often, the issue with these giant binders is that despite all the money and all the effort expended for their creation (and hopefully testing and validation), companies typically did not continually update them as their IT environments changed from month-to-month and year-to-year. However, true Disaster Recovery capability involves more than just maintaining the accuracy of the Binders. If changes are made to production, including new servers, software or storage architecture, then the Recovery Site would need those new items as well.

Virtualization changed all of that - for the good. Remember when I mentioned that Virtualizing a Server essentially converts all the factors of the server to a file (or a snapshot), including hardware, software, settings, etc., and that it runs on a Hypervisor? Since the Hypervisor handles the interaction of the virtual servers with the underlying hardware in the physical hosts, it is able to normalize those interactions to a common set of commands that work on almost any physical Resource Pool. Think of it as a translator of sorts that can take in any language and convert it to whatever language the Host computers are running.

Since the Virtual Server is a portable file, in that it can be copied, you don't need to worry about having those massive configuration binders to create the servers in the Recovery Site. You just need snapshot copies of the Virtual Server, with replicated data in the Recovery Site, and you are over halfway to bringing your firm's IT systems back online. A plan and appropriate documentation are still required, but they will be dramatically smaller and much more effective.

DESKTOP VIRTUALIZATION

There are several types of "Desktop Virualization." One of simplest forms is taking your PC and converting that machine's Operating System, application software, and its settings into a Virtual PC. Some people will choose to run Windows software on a Mac if they are dealing with software that will only run on a Windows system. A great example is running web systems that only run well in Internet Explorer, which is a Windows-based browser, and not as well in Safari. Microsoft OneNote is a fantastic note taking application that unfortunately is only available on Windows. What some people do is virtualize their Windows Desktop to run Explorer or One Note in a Mac Environment.

Another basic example of Desktop Virtualization is used by developers who have to run several versions of Windows at the same time, or a consultant who has to run a unique desktop for three different customers operating on different systems. They can virtualize each desktop so it may run on any system. Let's say one business customer uses Windows XP and another Windows 7 and another Windows 8. If you have to work with all of those in the same office environment, the consultant can take this "snapshot" and run each one on the same laptop. It's a very handy concept that relieves someone from having to pollute their own desktop operating system or carry three separate laptops to work each day.

The last type of desktop virtualization is called VDI (Virtual Desktop Infrastructure). VDI enables employees to use the same virtual desktop (that is stored on the main server) on a variety of machines or thin-client terminals. Say you have a bank where the tellers all use the same software applications. Their terminals all connect to a virtual desktop in the computer room, so the individual tellers don't need to worry about losing any data if their terminal should break. Further, this approach allows team members to move from location to location, providing seamless access to the same desktop. As an example, on day one a teller is working at Station A in the company headquarters. The very next day they travel to another regional office and log-in to Station B. Simply by using their personal log-in credentials, the very same user experience is achieved by maintaining the same desktop experience in the background. Many Universities and other schools use VDI for their students and faculty.

One obvious advantage is the retaining of all user data within your central computer room and not on the workstation's hard drive, which is more prone to failures. In addition, there are always concerns about laptop and desktop computer theft, raising the concern of personal information and sensitive data loss. However, utilizing a VDI strategy, the data can always be locked away securely on a server, and the workstations that access it never locally store that data. So if a laptop or terminal is stolen, it is essentially an empty computer, from a sensitive data perspective.

HOW CAN A BUSINESS OWNER IMPLEMENT VIRTUALIZATION?

Generally, server virtualization is not something you can easily buy or implement from a retail store because it's a technology that requires a specialist. On the other hand, that doesn't necessarily mean it takes a massive investment to accomplish.

Regardless of what you may be told, server virtualization is not something you should implement on your own. Businesses that try to tackle it themselves, without having staff with real virtualization architecture experience, inevitably create a bigger mess than what they started with. Usually this results in the creation of unplanned downtime that cannot be resolved until a professional can step in to fix it. It's the same reason I don't try doing my own plumbing work at my home.

What you should do is find a firm with specialists who have dozens of virtualization projects under their belts, as opposed to just a general IT guy who is learning virtualization as a small component of their overall IT knowledge. That is like asking a family physician to do brain surgery.

You should make sure the specialist you engage has acceptable credentials in implementing virtualization, preferably in your specific industry and with companies of your same size. They're not hard to find, but there are also plenty of charlatans out there that you need to avoid. Many of these charlatans are happy to take on your virtualization project so that they can learn how to do it. You don't want a rookie building such a critical system. The risks are far too high.

In addition, ask the prospective IT provider to furnish 4 or 5 references, of similar-sized projects, who are willing to accept a 20-30 minute phone call to discuss the project, and their quality of work, in great detail. At our firm, we could easily provide over thirty references if a client asks for them.

Besides the general questions regarding overall project success and client satisfaction, you want to make sure the firm you are considering took a methodical approach to the virtualization project. For example, any competent virtualization consultant should conduct a **discovery analysis** of the existing environment before determining how to configure the host resource pool. Generally, a simple 30-day performance data gathering would provide adequate information that could be used as an input to the **design phase**, which is another key function that the consultant should provide. Next, the consultant should **build** and **test** the configuration before migrating any production systems. Testing is crucial – both before and after the production systems are migrated. Our firm regularly receives calls to review poor performing or unreliable virtual systems and most often we find that the firm that implemented it failed to properly architect, implement and test the systems. Failure to plan, failure to analyze what is needed (i.e., how much horsepower it would take to run the virtual servers in the resource pool), and inadequate testing can all limit or prevent the success of your company's virtualization implementation. A strong virtualization implementation firm will help you avoid those headaches.

HANG IN THERE, VIRTUALIZATION IS WORTH IT!

Although Virtualization seems like an advanced technical topic, there is quantifiable ROI that business owners can experience by implementing Server Virtualization – which will help protect the firm from down-time while saving the firm money. Ten years ago, it was estimated that less than one third of Fortune 500 companies were using virtualization, but today **100 percent** use it in some way, shape or form. Best of all, small-to-medium sized businesses can take advantage of this ever-evolving technological marvel without breaking the bank. More companies than ever are adopting a "virtual-first" philosophy for their servers. If you haven't considered it, it is time to do so.

About John

John Biglin is a seasoned business executive and board-level advisor who leverages his 27 years of technology industry experience to help senior executives establish the ideal balance between performance, reliability, security, compliance and cost. Using a "Business-First" philosophy, John focuses on solving business needs rather than simply prescribing a particular technology.

John has a long history of launching, developing and managing several successful multi-million dollar firms, while helping other business owners do the same.

John is currently the Chief Executive Officer of Interphase Systems, Inc., a premier Technology and Managed Services firm serving the Life Sciences, Financial Services, Professional Services, Healthcare, Manufacturing, and other industries. Interphase Systems was founded in 1995 and has offices in Plymouth Meeting, PA and Bedminster, NJ.

After 20 years of working directly with Life Sciences firms, John pioneered the creation of Ready-IT BioPharma™, the Life Science Industry's first turnkey IT Service Platform that integrates core business and IT systems combined with support services, disaster recovery and regulatory compliance. His firm has since expanded the Ready-IT™ concept to other industries and integrated Cloud technologies into the service.

John's prior experience includes working as a senior consultant with IBM Corporation as well as other IT leadership positions. He has also been an adjunct professor of Business at Gwynedd Mercy College in Southeastern Pennsylvania.

John is regularly interviewed by major industry trade publications (*PharmaVoice, Pharmaceutical Commerce, eWeek, infoWorld, Technically Philly, etc.*) and has been a speaker at industry conferences, including:

- Virtualization Exchange (Keynote Speaker)
- Virtualization Technology Conference
- Philadelphia Cloud Computing Conference

John holds a Bachelor's degree in Computer Science from Rutgers University and an MBA from Penn State University.

CHAPTER 13

DISASTER RECOVERY

BY KEVIN JUSTUS

Disaster Recovery is one of those topics that most business owners put on the back burner of their priority list. There are numerous reasons they procrastinate when it comes to nailing down a specific plan as it pertains to their business. One of the main reasons is that Disaster Recovery is a large topic with so many potential components that many people don't even know where to begin. In fact, you will discover that the subject matter in this chapter will overlap other topics in this book because of its breadth.

If you think "data backup" is synonymous with "disaster recovery" and you aren't sure what "business continuity" means, you're not alone. Most of the business owners I talk to make the sometimes disastrous mistake of not knowing the difference. Unfortunately, they end up paying the price when data is lost, a network goes down, or a disaster prevents them from accessing their physical office and the server lying inside a burned-out building, or a building demolished by a tornado or hurricane.

Of course, not all disasters are of hurricane proportions. In the grand scheme of things and for the purposes of this chapter, a disaster can range from malfunctioning software caused by a computer virus to a situation as devastating as all of your data and every last piece of equipment owned by your business being destroyed in some catastrophic manner.

This subject has received a high degree of attention in the press as well as by lawmakers over the past twenty years. The major catastrophes leading this concentration of thought include the 1993 bombing of the World Trade Center; the 1995 bombing of the Federal Building in Oklahoma City; and the unthinkable terrorist attack on the World Trade Center that changed the course of our nation's history. Add to these devastating events the countless hurricanes and tornadoes that have wreaked havoc on homes and businesses in numerous states and you can understand why so much has been said in the last two decades about disaster recovery.

THE DIFFERENCE BETWEEN DATA BACKUP, DISASTER RECOVERY AND BUSINESS CONTINUITY

Before moving too far into this chapter, it will be important to define Disaster Recovery and how it differs from Data Backup and Business Continuity as it relates to your business. Here are the definitions that will bring some distinction between them for the purposes of this chapter.

Data Backup simply means that a copy of your data is replicated to another device or location. Sources such as tape drives, offsite backup and even USB devices provide data backup. While data backup is obviously important, another equally important consideration is whether or not your backup solution provides easy recovery.

Business Continuity is the ability of your business to continue to operate even after a major disaster. For example, if you ran an accounting firm and your building burned to the ground, you'd be out of business if all your files were on the server only. However, if you had your network in the cloud, your employees could continue to work from home or some other location, giving your business "continuity."

Disaster Recovery is the ability of your business to "recover" after the occurrence of a disaster. It is the capacity to recover all your files, software and business functionality quickly, easily and without corruption. For example, if your server died, you wouldn't be able to get back to work quickly if you only had a file-level backup. In order to start working again, your server would need to be replaced, your software would need to be reinstalled and your data would need to be restored. Then, the whole system would need to be reconfigured with your settings and preferences. This process could take hours or even days—and that's if you have all your software licenses and a clean copy of your data. The subject of Disaster Recovery can have far-reaching implications depending upon the extent of the "disaster" from which you need to recover.

WILL DISASTER STRIKE YOUR BUSINESS?

Obviously, the answer to this question is unknown. However, while we don't know if or when disaster may strike, there is no doubt that every business must have a plan to recover from a catastrophic event. Consider these statistics from various studies that have been completed related to this subject.

- According to a study conducted by Chubb, 70% of businesses involved in a major fire fail within 3 years.

- AXA reports that one out of two businesses never return to the marketplace following a major disaster.

- The National Archives and Records Administration provides information indicating that 93% of companies that lost their data for 10 days or more filed for bankruptcy within one year of the disaster and 50% filed for bankruptcy immediately.

If you are a business owner, these statistics should cause you to sit up and take notice. You may find it shocking to know that, according to FEMA, within two years after Hurricane Andrew in Florida (1992), 80% of affected companies that lacked a disaster recovery plan went out of business. Further information gleaned from a report by Gartner reveals that only 35% of small to medium-sized businesses have a comprehensive disaster recovery plan in place.

ARE YOU READY FOR A DISASTER?

Disasters come in various forms and each can create their unique level of devastation. Here is a short list of events that could be problematic or even cause business failure if you are not properly prepared:

- Flood
- Fire
- Natural Disaster (hurricane, tornado, earthquake, tsunami, etc.)
- Major power outage

- Internal Sabotage
- Medical Emergency (widespread epidemic)
- Hardware Failure
- Chemical Spill
- Gas Line Explosion

Given the human tendency to be optimistic and always look on the bright side, many business owners are prone to ignore the implementation of a Disaster Recovery Plan because any kind of catastrophic event seems highly unlikely. Unfortunately, this type of lack of concern and inept foresight has caused many good businesses to dissolve because they were not able to recover after a significant disruption. For the sake of your business and your employees, don't allow your business to be caught unprepared.

DEVELOP A COMPREHENSIVE DISASTER RECOVERY PLAN

Your Disaster Recovery Plan will require a significant amount of thought and time for it to be effective. The following suggestions will help you in this process.

• Create a Written Plan

- As simple as it may sound, just thinking through and writing down in ADVANCE what needs to happen if your server has a meltdown or a natural disaster wipes out your office, will go a long way in getting your business back online fast. There are no "cookie cutter" templates for this process. While there are some common elements among plans, every organization's plan will be different because every business has needs that are specific and unique. Depending on the size and complexity of your company, you will likely have to include numerous people in the planning process. If it makes sense for the size of your company, create a Disaster Recovery Team that will work together to develop a cohesive plan and will be committed to updating the plan and keeping all employees prepared.

• Think Business Continuity Not Just Data Backup

- A HUGE mistake made by almost all business owners is thinking that having a backup copy of your data will enable you to be back in business quickly. That is very far from the truth! Even if you have all your data restored, if you don't have a place for employees to work, for example, because your building has been destroyed, it is likely you will not be able to do anything with the restored data. You must think in terms of, "How will my business continue to provide products or services to my customers after suffering a catastrophic event?" "What must I do to minimize the disruption to my business, my customers and my cash flow?"

- **Documentation**
  - Network documentation is simply a blueprint of the software, data, systems and hardware you have in your company's network. Your IT manager or IT consultant should put this together for you and it should include all of your equipment and software with serial numbers. But don't stop there. Make sure to include documentation about your key vendors, how to shut off the gas and water, numbers for emergency services, etc. You also must document the specific responsibilities individuals within your organization will have should an event occur. Who will they call? Who must be notified and who will do the notification? What are the first steps they will take? If it is a larger company with numerous employees and there are multiple exits from your building, what exit should each employee use for an emergency evacuation? Where will employees go when they evacuate the building? Who will be responsible for accounting for all employees if a building evacuation is necessary? Who will "sweep" the building to make sure everyone is out safely? As you can see, the list of documented items must be very detailed. Any missed steps could not only cost you monetarily, it could also cost lives.

- **Test**
  - The only way to know if you have a good plan is to test it. Don't wait for a disaster to find out you missed a major business function within your plan. Make sure everyone has a copy of the plan and conduct drills so everyone is aware of their roles and responsibilities in case of a disaster. Every person who has a role in the plan must have a copy of the Disaster Recovery Plan

to which they can refer at the time of an event. In fact, it is a good idea for them to have a plan in their desk as well as in their vehicle or at home. Keep in mind that it will be easy for people to forget their roles and responsibilities, so it will be a good idea to revisit the plan on a regular basis. I recommend revisiting the plan with your staff on a quarterly or semi-annual basis.

People within your organization need to comprehend the great importance of this issue and their role in enabling the business to recover. Every employee should have an understanding of what they need to do in case of a disaster. Items that should be covered with employees include, but are not limited to, the following: Individual roles and responsibilities; information about threats, hazards and protective actions; notification, warning and communications procedures; emergency response procedures; evacuation and use of common emergency equipment; and emergency shutdown procedures. Your Disaster Recovery Plan should also be part of the new employee orientation so they understand what they need to do if an event should occur.

• Update Often

- If the information in the plan is not up to date, it is useless. Make sure you update the information monthly or at least quarterly. Your business probably changes much more often than you realize. When changes are made in your business or when new equipment and software is added, make sure you update your written Disaster Recovery Plan accordingly. Then, make sure everyone who has a role in your recovery plan receives an updated copy of the written plan.

Disaster Recovery and emergency preparedness should not be an option in your business. No matter the size of your business, it should be a "must have" component. It should be a subject built into the very culture of your organization. When it comes to protecting your company and keeping your operations running, you need to know for certain—without any lingering doubts—that your business could continue running during and after a natural disaster, server crash, hacker attack or other type of event.

About Kevin

Kevin Justus began taking electronics apart as a child and putting them back together for fun. When he got his first computer, he moved to the next best thing.

In 2001, Kevin started Shoreline Information Technologies and his hobby became his life's work. In 2010, Kevin joined an IT industry group with global membership that covers a wide range of topics in business and technology.

His mission is simple: make technology an asset for your business, not a liability. This means he helps each client leverage technology to increase their bottom line profits, rather than technology slowing them down or getting in the way altogether.

In 2011, he wrote a book entitled, *Computers Should Just Work* which talks about what business owners should expect from IT service providers, and how to choose the right one. The second edition with updated information about the latest technology will be published in 2014.

Kevin lives and works in Santa Cruz County with his wife and 3 children.

Contact information – visit my website at: shorelineit.com/book
or by calling 831-708-3140 or by emailing me at: info@shorelineit.com.

****

ADDENDUM

Today's businesses require a better backup solution. With more data being created, the value of the data increasing, stricter regulations, and no time for downtime—an image-based backup solution fits the bill better than older, outdated methods.

With image-based backup a picture of the workstation or server is taken and stored as a place in time for that machine. This is essential for restoration because rebuilding or virtualizing a machine requires not just files but also the applications and systems. Backups are the size of the changed data between two points but hold the information to restore any piece of data that was on the machine at the time of the backup.

Additional advantages of image-based backup are: full restores are faster, can restore individual files, ability for bare metal restores (BMR), can verify images, boot virtual machines, and run remote offices.

datto

CHAPTER 14

TOTAL COST OF OWNERSHIP

BY LAUREN GROFF

There are numerous ways to evaluate the cost of ownership related to the Information Technology (IT) of your business. In fact, many vendors have very extensive spreadsheets to measure your Return on Investment (ROI) for a given piece of hardware or software. This chapter, however, will look at a cohesive approach to determining the overall cost of technology as compared to the cost of NOT having the right systems, processes, AND people in place.

How much do you value technology? How much do you value the time of your employees? How committed are you to increasing your revenue and profit margin and reducing expenses? Your answer to these questions will have a tremendous impact on your overall business and technology planning strategy. That is, IF your business model includes dependence upon technology. If your computers can run slowly, or you can turn them off for a few hours, AND it doesn't affect your company's ability to perform, then your business is probably NOT all that dependent upon technology and you can skip to the next chapter.

A number of years ago, I purchased a 1994 Honda Accord because of the vehicle's reputation of dependability and longevity. It was a great car and I was committed to driving it until the wheels fell off. After 14 years of reliable service from my beloved Accord, I began to feel the economic pinch of maintaining a vehicle that seemed to be about a decade older than every other car on the road. As with any vehicle of that age, things began wearing out. The ball joints had to be replaced, the brake rotors were shot, engine oil was leaking, the power steering fluid was leaking everywhere, who knows what was making a clanking noise, and the list goes on. In addition to that, I had to consider the safety of my family. A failing ball joint can bring your car to a rapid halt in the middle of an Interstate. I eventually arrived at the reluctant conclusion that it was costing me more money to hold on to the Accord than it was to buy a new vehicle and my growing family's protection was of utmost importance. I EVEN ALMOST MISSED AN APPOINTMENT WITH AN IMPORTANT PROSPECT BECAUSE OF AN ISSUE WITH BRAKE LINES. It was starting to cost me more than just money out of my pocket for repairs. The day of ultimate decision came when I purchased a new vehicle without constant failure issues and I felt much more secure knowing my family was protected by the latest and greatest vehicle safety technology.

I share this story with you because I find the same issues facing business owners when it comes to the maintenance and longevity of their Information Technology (IT) infrastructure. Just as there are hard costs (insurance, maintenance, etc.) and less concrete costs (safety of your family) involved with owning an automobile, there are hard costs and less concrete costs to owning and operating the technology that supports your ongoing business.

And really, this is a lousy example, because it applies only if you are trying to solve the question of whether to replace the computers and servers sooner or later.

But we have to start somewhere.

Consider this, if you are using old and outdated IT infrastructure and equipment, you may be spending more money than you realize. There are costs to maintain old servers and old computers. Hardware issues cause productivity downtime which can translate into lost data, lost time, lost sales, customer dissatisfaction and employee frustration, to name only a few. Depending on your business, an antiquated IT infrastructure could literally cost you tens of thousands of dollars every year to keep running, which is MORE than the cost if you were to simply replace them and achieve the otherwise missed benefits. But that's just the beginning of the considerations.

Perception has a lot to do with how we view IT costs. Some business owners take the band-aid approach and keep patching and fixing old technology because they believe it is SAVING THEM MONEY. However, the very opposite is most likely true.

Let's use a picture to illustrate this. The circles below serve to demonstrate this point. Look at each center circle and then determine which circle is larger: the center circle on the left or the center circle on the right?

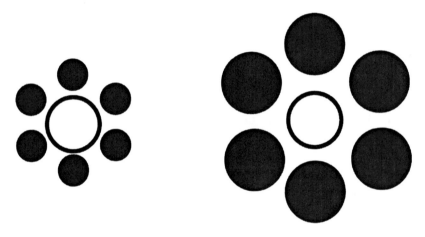

Most people determine that the center circle on the left is larger. If you haven't seen this illustrated before, you may be surprised to know that both center circles are exactly the same size. This is the same for your IT costs. For example, if you see spending more to get the right maintenance in place is expensive because, you think, "Hey if I can get the cheaper option, then I save money, right?" **But you don't get to choose the cost of your technology**. You can choose where you spend it though, AND you can choose to have the most effective, least overall cost. However, the only way to get that is to put the right support plan, team, process, investments, etc., in place.

COUNTING THE COST

Let's look at some of the other costs. For one, you may have someone in your office who is a "jack of all trades." That's the individual who knows how to clear the paper jams in the copy machine, track down viruses that have been introduced to your computers, and is the "go-to" guy or gal for everything technical in your office. However, usually that individual has a main responsibility, often marketing or finance, that he or she is being pulled from to answer the countless questions and deal with the multitude of technology mishaps occurring every month. How much is that person's non-productivity costing you because they are being pulled in multiple directions to help everyone else? How much marketing is NOT being done because that person is fixing computers?

Then there is the cost of not having the right preventative systems in place. If your time spent on tech issues per computer user in your office is, let's say, 3 hours per month, that far exceeds the best of class industry standard of 15 to 30 minutes per month. That is at least 6 times as much downtime per employee. By multiplying the number of employees by the number of hours spent on tech issues, then multiplying that times their hourly wage, you can see how costly that can become. Then you must add in the cost of how that time affects your revenue, lost sales, potentially disgruntled customers and employee morale.

For example, let's consider the scenario of a 25-employee business with an annual average wage of $40,000 per employee. Add something like an additional 25% for benefits (payroll taxes, insurance, etc.) and that is an additional $10,000 per employee. That is an annual payroll of $1,250,000 ($50,000 x 25), or just over $600 per hour. If your technology is down, or even just slow, for 3 hours per month, it is costing you over $1,800 per month in employee costs ALONE, compared to having the right support system and technology in place. Add to this scenario how their productivity is tied to revenue, a much harder number to calculate, but we know that it is a much larger number. You can easily see how costly your IT downtime or slowness can become.

But you might say, I don't believe that I have that much slowness or downtime. In my experience, if you don't have a ticketing system or report telling you how many issues are reported and how much time per issue, then you can, out-of-the-gate, assume at least 2 hours of *preventable* issues per employee per month.

STRATEGIC TECHNOLOGY PLANNING

If your company isn't doing technology planning, there is a high likelihood that your equipment is outdated and it's costing you money that you don't realize. The big question that faces most business owners is, "Do I try to get by with my 6-year old server and my 5-year old computers or do I invest in new, more efficient technology?"

But that is just scratching the surface of the benefits of strategic planning. Some more important questions where technology can be a very large factor are:

- Where is your business headed?
- What opportunities will you only be able to leverage with the addition or change of technology?
- Where can you reduce costs?

Lacking in any of these areas may cost one business a little, but others a lot. But for many business owners, who want to take their business places and do so profitably, this is crucial as technology becomes ever more integral in the running and achieving success as a small business.

Add to the list, for example, potential productivity gains, from receiving true help from a partner who understand general business principals, and more importantly, your business specifically, yet can apply technology insight to help you in that process. If you are lacking that, what is that opportunity cost to you?

DISASTER RECOVERY PLANNING

Disaster Recovery Planning is another crucial consideration when it comes to assessing your cost of doing business. For example, if no one is monitoring your back up data and you lose data over a period of time, there is a cost that can be associated with that loss. In an extreme case, it could put you out of business. Spending a few hundred dollars on a reliable backup system is much more cost efficient than losing data that could potentially cost you AT LEAST tens of thousands of dollars. In general, you must ask yourself the question, "What is the cost of not having the right systems in place or the right support and maintenance of your infrastructure?" If you are not 100% sure you could get back in the event of a failure or disaster, what is the COST to your business of carrying that risk?

A server failure, even with a good backup of your DATA, could literally mean 2 to 3 days of downtime for your entire office. Without the right systems and support in place, it is very likely you will lose your server over the course of time. It usually isn't a matter of "if" you will lose it, it's a matter of "when" you will lose it. Most small businesses will experience a major data loss within a 10-year period of time. For those who did not properly prepare, this would be quite costly. Using the payroll figures from earlier, if you have a 3-day outage, your cost will be nearly $15,000 just in payroll. And again, you would have to add to that number the loss of revenue to your business during this 3-day period. And that's not even taking into consideration if you can't recover that data! Backup routines break ALL THE TIME. Compare this scenario to having the right support model and system in place, which would enable you to be back up and running within 2 to 3 hours, or for some systems, 2-3 minutes. As you can see, the cost savings simply by initiating proper planning can be crucial to your business.

VIRUSES, SPAM BOTS AND CRYPTOLOCKER, OH MY!

By not having the proper security in place you subject your computers to becoming infected with dangerous viruses and spam bots that can prove to be hazardous in several ways. Cryptolocker, for example, can lock down much of your critical data until you pay a $300 ransom. Protecting yourself from items like this will be addressed in the chapter on Data Security. Let's just say that if you don't spend the money to protect your network, these infiltrations can be VERY costly to your business.

IN-HOUSE IT STAFF OR OUTSOURCING YOUR IT NEEDS

Of course there is the cost of the IT services itself. Some decide that they've grown enough to hire a full-time IT person. This is a challenge in a small business, because what do you hire for? You have at least three different levels of expertise and skill that one needs to supply for. At the first level, most of the labor of IT is day-to-day user support. Yet the most important is the care of the network, **regardless of whether you are in the cloud or not**. This second level of course requires a higher skillset. Then the third level is the strategic consulting. Let's not forget that most businesses have a person, whether internal or outsourced, manually implementing patches, fixes, etc. These sorts of things can be EASILY automated with the right tools and dedication. Obviously, the right technology partner already has built these and can just drop them in place in a new network.

When you properly outsource your IT, you get everything you need. Whether or not you have internal IT staff. You receive a higher level of expertise, day-to-day support (or backup support if you have internal IT staff), strategy and maintenance balance. However, finding the right system and partner is quite difficult to do because they aren't plentiful.

There are two basic philosophies held by IT vendors. The first is the idea that you just chase the problems. Some vendors build their entire company around that philosophy. However, it can become a spiral of death for an IT company because it means they need enough fires to keep them in business, but they can't afford to have all those fires burning at once. And while chasing urgent issues, there is absolutely not enough time spent dedicated to all of the important maintenance, the network analysis, the security monitoring, etc. that need to be a priority in order to keep the negative impact of technology low. Unfortunately, you may call an IT company like this and not get them on the phone because they are chasing someone else's fire.

The second philosophical approach is to take a proactive stance. Now don't get me wrong, this is the TALK of a lot of IT companies. However, this is very difficult to actually do. For one, to truly 'do' proactive well, there are a myriad of systems and processes that have to be developed. **The average 'proactive' IT business is just charging a monthly fee for you to retain them to be reactive.** There is a large challenge with belief systems as well. Charging the right amount AND saying 'NO' to distractions is very hard for an owner of a small IT business, or any owner for that matter. And usually, if an IT company has ever been break-fix, **it takes about 3 years** to make the move from a reactive model to become truly proactive – and most don't make that transition. Remember, it's VERY hard to dedicate the hard work to prevent problems when another client is demanding attention right now for their reactive problem. I strongly believe a business must be prepared to move from a reactive to a proactive approach when it comes to their IT infrastructure and they must realize the old adage is very true, "you get what you pay for." The cost of NOT having the right partner in place usually oozes out all over the place, and most small business owners think they are OK with it, as long as their IT people fix stuff and show up on time. But as we've seen from our treatment of this topic so far,[1] **this** can be the most costly (if you get it wrong) or cost-effective (if you get it right) decision, as it drives all of the other costs above.

The following diagram is an example of how IT costs stack up, particularly when "hard" costs are held artificially low, compared to spending the right amount on keeping the overall technology costs minimized.

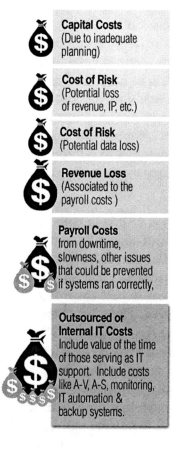

Capital Costs
(Due to inadequate planning)

Cost of Risk
(Potential loss of revenue, IP, etc.)

Cost of Risk
(Potential data loss)

Revenue Loss
(Associated to the payroll costs)

Payroll Costs
from downtime, slowness, other issues that could be prevented if systems ran correctly,

Outsourced or Internal IT Costs
Include value of the time of those serving as IT support. Include costs like A-V, A-S, monitoring, IT automation & backup systems.

Spending The Right Amount
Spending the right amount (Requires the right systems, process and people)

---

1. We haven't exhausted the realm of technology cost analysis; there simply isn't enough room in this short treatise to do so.

PLAN, PLAN, PLAN

You must ask yourself the following questions:

"If I am not doing everything I could be doing to apply technology in a greater and more beneficial way to my business, what am I missing out on?"

"What is the cost to my business by not having the right technology strategy in place?"

If you are hap-hazardly following marketing trends and if you don't have a strategic consultant or partner in the area of technology, then what is that costing your business?

A qualified IT consulting firm is not just someone who is fixing stuff and calling it 'consulting'. They are a firm who truly understands business and helps not just untangle the question of which piece of hardware to buy and when, but an outfit that can spend the time to *understand* your business and can *research and advise* and bring solutions to the table that can HELP your business. A firm that can truly deliver this becomes not just a cost that can be minimized, but, and those who receive this know this is true, *a resource to invest in that yields DIVIDENDS.*

So it's up to you, do you want to just spend less for someone to fix stuff? Or, do you want to spend less money in your *business overall* by leveraging technology to reduce costs, increase profit and increase revenues?

About Lauren

Lauren Groff is dedicated to helping businesses get the technology they need to achieve their business goals. After working as a Computer and Network Administrator for over five years and being downsized twice, he decided to go out on his own. He was a one-man band, fixing computers in his living room when he started Groff NetWorks in 2005. Today, Groff NetWorks is one of the leading providers of Managed Services and Computer Support in New York's Capital Region, serving businesses throughout Albany, Troy, Schenectady, Latham, Saratoga Springs and Clifton Park.

Lauren's company is centered on his philosophy of personalized service. Groff NetWorks prides itself on delivering honest, reliable, high-quality service and values their partnerships with clients. When you call Groff NetWorks for help, you get a personable and professional IT expert to answer all of your questions, not an automated 1-800 number. Lauren fully considers each client's bottom line, budget, and expectations while strengthening their infrastructure to boost their productivity and profitability. Groff's technology solutions are always customized to meet their clients' needs. This philosophy has helped Lauren to emerge into new markets and build business relationships at an exponential rate.

Lauren graduated *Cum Laude* from Colgate University with a Bachelor of Arts in Philosophy and Religion. He also proudly holds the prestigious Eagle Scout rank from the Boy Scouts of America. As an active member of and former ambassador for the Rensselaer County Regional Chamber of Commerce, he graduated from the Chamber's SmartUp business program and The Leadership Institute. He later appeared as a guest on Chamber Chat on NewsTalk1300. He is a winner of Master Schnizzer 2013 (TruMethods), and Marketing Genius of the month (TMT); he was a finalist in the Better Your Best contest (TMT) and was recognized by The Albany Business Review as a 40 under 40 winner.

Lauren is an enthusiastic and active member of his community. Lauren served as an adjunct instructor at ITT Technical Institute in Latham, and he currently sits on the technical advisory board at Mildred Elley School of Business and Technology in Albany. He is the former President of the Downtown Troy Business Improvement District, which he helped launch and still participates as a board member. Lauren has been featured in local newspapers, magazines and news channels. He is a volunteer for Joseph's House Inn From The Cold and an active member at Terra Nova Church. He, his wife and their four children live in and love historic downtown Troy, NY!

You can connect with Lauren at:
lgroff@groffnetworks.com
www.groffnetworks.com

CHAPTER 15

CLOUD COMPUTING

BY LLIAM AND JENNIFER HOLMES

Cloud computing is gaining traction with business owners because it offers potential for reduced costs, improved efficiency, flexibility, and "anywhere, anytime" access to company applications.

Many of today's business owners are faced with the arduous task of evaluating the cloud as it pertains to their needs. Unfortunately, most don't know enough about cloud computing or how it's different from what they have today. They are further confused by advocates highlighting virtues and advantages, while others sound alerts about potential hazards.

What is cloud computing? When does cloud computing offer opportunities for small- to medium-sized businesses? What does it cost? How do you identify an experienced cloud provider from a startup? This chapter answers these questions to help business owners understand the cloud, where it potentially fits in their businesses and how it can create a competitive advantage.

DEFINING THE CLOUD

Realistically, cloud computing is not new technology, but a collection of technologies that have been in the market space for a long time. The cloud is really a different way of selling — just re-branding and re-packaging this technology.

When you research cloud computing among technology providers, you find highly variable definitions. This allows cloud providers to bend and redefine the definition for their own purposes and marketing edge, further adding to prospects' confusion. However, in its purest form, the cloud is simply having a set of servers in a data center. It is a subscription-based model of computing that allows you to pay only for what you use without ever having to worry about buying or maintaining new servers or Microsoft software (Windows and Office). It's a scalable, "pay-as-you-go" and "pay-as-you-grow" strategy.

In general, there are three basic categories: the public cloud, the private cloud and the hybrid cloud. While providers may use other names for their services, it all comes back to these categories. Before making a decision about cloud computing, a business owner needs to understand how the three differ and know that all clouds are not created equal in terms of cost, security, flexibility and choice.

I. The Public Cloud

In the public cloud, multiple servers are housed in a secure data center and shared by many companies, with access to applications and data through the Internet. Configuration decisions made in a public cloud space are standardized to lower costs and increase scalability for the cloud provider. This resource sharing offers the advantage of lower costs for everyone. However, everything has to be configured to meet the criteria of the lowest common denominator among all the participants. This results in limited choice and flexibility because each participating company cannot customize its own servers, security and system resources. For example, if one provider wants to use a certain type of spam filter, then that's the spam filter everyone must use. If a customer doesn't like that spam filter, then they will have to go outside that cloud solution to find what they want — and then their preferred solution may or may not be supported by the public cloud. Because everyone has to share common computing resources and infrastructure, everyone can't have their own customizations. Obviously, this doesn't work for all, but it does offer a low-cost entry point for services. If you are looking for basic services, require few customizations and an easy way to get started, the public cloud may be a fit for you.

Some businesses have very specific configuration or software needs and find that the public cloud is not a viable option. Take the example of an insurance agency owner who came to us. His company used an agency management application that required a certain version of Microsoft Office. When their public cloud provider upgraded Microsoft Office, it broke their main agency software, resulting in a major business interruption. To help get what they needed, we transitioned them from a public cloud provider to a private cloud provider, which gave them the flexibility to choose the version of Microsoft Office they could run.

II. The Private Cloud

The private cloud is exactly the opposite of the public cloud. In the private cloud, a company's servers are housed in a secure data center and are dedicated only to that company, again with access over the Internet. The servers are assigned and configured to one particular customer and only that company's data. They don't share their servers with anyone else and their data never comingles with other firms' information. Companies use a private cloud if they want flexibility to add specific applications, upgrade a particular version of software or if they don't want to upgrade it on a mandated schedule. The server configuration and the application settings are completely customizable for the individual company. They have the flexibility of controlling the servers to best accommodate their business needs. The flexibility of having a private cloud is a close approximation to having your own servers in your own building with all the benefits of cloud computing.

III. The Hybrid Cloud

Not every company fits into the public or private cloud model. Some companies need a combined configuration to accomplish their business goals. For them, a hybrid cloud solution may be the answer. In this scenario some business applications are well suited for a cloud environment, while others are designed more for an on-premise application. For example, a video production company may have certain applications that work well in the cloud, but other "resource-heavy" applications require a local server. Likewise, a design, marketing, construction or contracting firm using AutoCAD®-like applications, which also are resource-demanding, may not typically perform well in the cloud. However, applications serving other portions of their businesses — such as file sharing, email, accounting or the phone system — may fit nicely into these companies' cloud environments. A hybrid cloud solution makes sense for organizations that have a mixture of applications in which some are cloud suitable, while others are not and must remain local-server based.

IS THE CLOUD A GOOD FIT FOR YOUR BUSINESS?

Many businesses find the cloud to be advantageous, but it's not a good fit for all. The reasons for using or not using the cloud differ, based on business and application needs. Trigger events often drive companies to evaluate cloud-computing options. Common ones are rapid growth, expansion, opening new offices, and looking for ways to improve efficiency, productivity and flexibility through technology.

For some, it is mainly about budget. A business could face spending a lot of money to replace an outdated server, old computers and archaic software, which are adversely affecting efficiency or productivity. Instead of enduring the financial pain of laying out one large lump sum to change technology infrastructure, a cloud solution through a qualified provider would enable them to spread the capital outlay over a period of time. Another company could have another pressing expenditure requiring significant capital investment and they don't have the cash flow to change their aging technology at the same time.

Cloud computing also may be a smart choice for someone with a seasonal business. If part of the year they have to scale up to meet larger technology demand and then scale back for the remainder of the year, the cloud may be the perfect solution. It is scalable and can accommodate those fluctuating needs. Conversely, if they were to buy that infrastructure (computers, servers, storage devices, etc.), they would have to pay for that equipment whether or not they use it. So, from a purely economic standpoint, it would make sense to evaluate options with the cloud.

Another common trigger event for businesses in today's marketplace is compliance. More and more industries are becoming highly regulated in the areas of information security. Many businesses are becoming overwhelmed by compliance issues to the point that they are outsourcing much of their technology to experts. The knowledge it takes to be compliant, the applications needed and the necessary security measures are far more involved than the average business is able to handle independently. Fortunately, a cloud-computing solution from a qualified provider can become a lifesaver for these business owners.

As this trend continues, an increasing number of companies will depend on an outside specialist because they don't want to or don't know how to deal with the compliance nightmare they face. It won't be about cost, but just making sure it's done properly so they won't fall prey to costly fines and penalties for noncompliance or potential breaches. The cloud will allow them to get back to the core of their business rather than constantly chasing and worrying about compliance and security issues.

HOW MOBILITY IS DRIVING CLOUD COMPUTING

It is very easy to see how technology is rapidly changing people's lives. In 2003 there were 0.8 electronic devices for every man, woman and child on planet Earth. In 2010 it grew to 1.84 devices per person. By 2015 we expect that number to jump to a staggering 3.5. The wide use of smartphones, tablets and mobile devices is creating new challenges for companies. With employees bringing their own devices to work, employers must secure their networks against unauthorized access through these devices and also set acceptable use policies and processes to ensure data protection and security enforcement.

Securing the data on all those devices is resulting in new laws and regulations (especially regarding healthcare, insurance and financial services information) that are being pushed down to small and medium-sized businesses. A number of new laws have specific provisions about what to do if a regulated device is lost. Who is responsible for reporting the loss? Is the company responsible for being able to locate the device or being able to remotely wipe the device? If it isn't done, who has the fiduciary responsibility for that negligence? These are just some of the accountability issues that only five years ago didn't exist. This security exposure is creating a whole new industry called mobile device management.

When companies contemplate the responsibilities associated with these new regulations, they often conclude that it's going to be too expensive, they don't have the skill set, or it's not something they want to undertake. That becomes another driver pushing people to the cloud. The security and compliance piece then becomes part of the service offered by the cloud provider, helping take some of the burden off the customer.

HOW CLOUD COMPUTING COST IS CALCULATED

Operationally mature cloud providers typically charge on a "per-user" basis, ranging from $70 to $350 per user per month. The main variables affecting per-user price include the types of applications, data storage/

size requirements, data retention periods, security measures, complexity of your environment, services that are bundled with cloud computing power, number of servers, availability of multiple data centers, disaster recovery options, and compliance levels. This fixed-fee approach makes pricing transparent and monthly bills predictable.

Other cloud providers price on a "per-user-plus-cost" model that includes the above variables plus other costs. The "plus costs" may include items such as bandwidth usage, power consumption, cooling requirements, failover capabilities and number of multiple Internet Service Providers available. These built-in, provider-based revenue "safety valves" make it difficult for companies to calculate usage and, therefore, their monthly costs. "Plus costs" can vary greatly from month to month, bringing unpredictability to your monthly cloud-computing bill.

CHOOSING THE RIGHT CLOUD PROVIDER

Cloud computing has become a growing segment over the last decade and especially within the last five years. Many service companies have sprung up to meet demand. A tremendous amount of responsibility falls upon the cloud provider. It must stay abreast of all technology and compliance issues, hire the right people, make sure staff is certified appropriately, be accountable for the safety of data, and the list goes on. Selecting a qualified cloud provider is critical.

The first problem that business owners face when they consider moving to the cloud is trying to buy a service they don't necessarily understand. This makes it difficult to compare providers. And, unlike highly regulated industries such as financial services, medicine or law, there are no Information Technology licensing requirements. If you go to a doctor, you know the physician had to graduate from an accredited medical school to practice medicine. You also know that your lawyer had to pass the state bar exam in order to practice law. Unfortunately, in IT that type of regulation doesn't exist.

How can you tell whether a prospective company is a quality provider? Below is a checklist of some basic questions to ask when choosing a qualified cloud provider for your business.

1. Does the provider share infrastructure or management with multiple third-party providers? Delivering reliable, stable, cloud-computing

environments is a complex process. Many smaller, less-experienced cloud providers rely on shared infrastructure and they license other providers to deliver services to their customers. This approach is risky because it removes the customer from having a direct relationship with these third-party providers. If there is a major problem, it leaves the customer without one source to "own the problem" and quickly identify and solve it. When interviewing a potential cloud provider, ask how many third-party vendors they rely upon and whether they built their own cloud. And, don't be afraid to ask why or why not. The answer will reveal the provider's skill level and help uncover any dependency risks that could limit your ability to get services or resolve problems that might occur.

2. Is the cloud provider a value-added "one-stop shop"? Anybody can call up a local cloud infrastructure provider, such as Rackspace, Amazon or Google, and contract for cloud computing services, virtual desktops, virtual servers, etc. for a customer. It is key to ask how integrations, upgrades, setup and maintenance will be performed and who will perform them. Will you have an assigned team to call or will your company be one of thousands of customers that have no assigned service team? Does the provider offer dedicated services such as help desk, backup disaster recovery, security audits, compliance, CIO level advisement, third-party application management, and local on-site support for your offices? It is important to understand the scope of what your provider offers and ensure it meets your support requirements.

3. What do new-customer onboarding and offboarding processes include? Ask the provider about the process for becoming a client. Who does what and when? Is the process explained in depth and with granularity covering things such as test environments, approval processes, go-live tests, training for staff, cutover details, stabilization periods, equipment compatibility, device minimum specifications, etc.? Should you decide to leave the provider, in what format would they provide your data — just the data, a copy of the virtual machines, an FTP site for file download, or just the most recent backup file? Ideally, the provider will give you a copy of your virtual machines in a standardized format within a defined timeframe, thereby making it easy for you to start with a new provider. Also, how long will it take to onboard or offboard? A reputable provider will spend from several

days to weeks onboarding, depending on your firm's complexity, and a similar amount of time for offboarding procedures. And one more very important question to ask: After you leave, will all of your data they held be erased so that it is not recoverable?

4. How is your data secured and protected? For example, you need to know exactly how your data is protected from equipment failures, including hardware, power, and Internet failures. How is your data segregated from other companies' data? What are the cloud provider's disaster recovery and business continuity procedures? Can they explain them in detail? Are they straightforward and easy to understand? How quickly can they get you back up and running if one of your virtual servers crashes? Does the provider's facility and staff meet HIPAA, PCI or other regulatory compliance and training requirements for your industry?

5. What does the service level agreement include? Reputable cloud providers define exactly what they will do, how and when they will do it, and what the client can expect, including uptime commitments and financial penalties for service unavailability. They also provide and describe guarantees for "time to first respond" for reported problems.

6. How would you be charged? Costs for cloud computing vary widely, based on your environment and requirements — plus whether the provider charges "per user", "per user plus cost" or a combination of both. To achieve a consistent, predictable monthly cost, select a provider that has a fixed-fee (per-user) approach, with minimal or no provider safety valves.

PARTNERING FOR SUCCESS IN THE CLOUD

We hope this chapter has helped you understand how you might be able to use cloud technology to cut costs and increase flexibility and access.

Knowing some of the basic questions to ask, you can look for a partner that is both qualified and dedicated to your company's success.

About Lliam and Jennifer

Lliam W. Holmes

Lliam's experience in the IT industry spans over 25 years. He has served as a field tech, systems engineer, project manager, software developer and business consultant for FORTUNE 500 companies and many other businesses (including Nokia Cellular, NAPA Auto Parts, Eli Lilly, HGTV, Crozer-Keystone Hospitals, Bethco Inc., Optima Technologies and BravePoint), and chief executive officer.

In 1995, Lliam founded MIS Solutions, Inc. in Suwanee, Ga., to help small Gwinnett County businesses leverage their technology to grow and achieve their goals. Today he architects Managed IT and Cloud strategies to help simplify technology, increase productivity and deliver a competitive edge for small companies in the Atlanta metro area — and through the addition of affiliate offices in Chicago, Las Vegas, Boston, Clarkston, Mass., and its partner network, MIS provides coverage in all 50 states. Gwinnett Magazine recognized MIS Solutions as "Best IT Service Provider" for seven consecutive years.

As MIS CEO, he focuses on strategic direction, research, development, operations and strategic business consulting, delivering innovative and creative solutions that tackle business owners' challenges. To help other IT companies, he works with a national operations group of managed IT and cloud service providers that creates network monitoring and issue remediation strategies. Rhodesian-born Lliam, his wife Jennifer and two children reside in Sugar Hill, Georgia.

For more information about MIS Solutions, visit: mis-solutions.com or email him at: lholmes@mis-solutions.com.

Jennifer L. Holmes

After graduating from Georgia Tech, Jennifer Holmes became an accomplished research virologist at the Centers for Disease Control and Prevention in Atlanta — where she submitted novel gene sequences to GenBank and published her scientific work in nationally recognized journals, including the Archives of Virology and the American Journal of Epidemiology. In 2000, this Georgia native hung up her lab coat to join husband Lliam at MIS Solutions, Inc., a Managed IT and Cloud Services company he founded that serves the Atlanta metro area and, through affiliate offices in the Chicago, Las Vegas, Boston, Clarkston, Massachusetts and its partner network, provides coverage throughout all 50 states.

As MIS President, she leads marketing, communications and business development, sharing effective business strategies to deliver the best business solutions for each client's unique environment and needs. Jennifer's leadership and marketing skills won her the title of 2013 Technology Marketing Toolkit Spokesperson for a nationally-acclaimed industry group of over 550 top U.S. IT experts who share best practices, marketing strategies, innovation and mentorship with computer and cloud service provider companies. This graduate of the Leadership Gwinnett program has acted on the boards of the National Association of Women Business Owners' Atlanta chapter, Gwinnett Great Days of Service, the Buford/North Gwinnett Rotary Club and the Gwinnett Chamber's Technology Board. Jennifer, Lliam and their children make their home in Sugar Hill, Georgia.

For more information about MIS Solutions, visit: mis-solutions.com or contact her at: jholmes@mis-solutions.com.

CHAPTER 16

HIPAA/MEDICAL

BY PETER VERLEZZA

If you have been to the doctor in the last few years you have heard of HIPAA. The Health Insurance Portability and Accountability ACT (HIPAA) was signed into law by President Bill Clinton on August 21, 1996. On January 25, 2013 a set of final regulations were published by the Department of Health and Human Services (HHS) called the HIPAA Omnibus Rule. We won't go into detail since the rules are complex. According to HHS, "The HIPAA Rules apply to **covered entities and business associates**." One type of Covered Entity is "A Health Care Provider" – Doctor, Clinic, Dentist, Nursing Home, Pharmacy, Psychologist, Chiropractor, etc. A Business Associate could be a Lawyer, Accountant, Answering Service, IT Company, Shredding or Storage Company, Medical Transcription Company, etc.

In this chapter we will discuss HIPAA, and more specifically, the HIPAA Security Rule, which deals with electronic protected health information (ePHI). The HIPAA Privacy Rule deals with all forms of patients' protected health information, electronic, written or oral. The HIPAA Security Rule is highly technical in nature, applies to both Covered Entities and Business Associates and will prove to be more challenging than the Privacy Rule.

The mandatory compliance date for the Omnibus Rule was September 23, 2013. However, in spite of this ruling, many Covered Entities and

Business Associates today are still not in compliance with HIPAA. There may be various reasons for these groups to defy their legal responsibility, but the law is still the law and it isn't a debatable issue.

I was recently asked to speak to a gathering of doctors and medical professionals. I gave the organizers of the event the following two titles I was considering for my presentation: "HIPAA: What is the Least Amount I Can Get Away With, Without Going to Jail?" Or "HIPAA: It's a Commandment Not a Suggestion." The organizers weren't overly fond of the first title, but were enthusiastic about the second one. However, at the risk of sounding too flippant (which isn't my intention), there are many medical practices that actually use the first title as their philosophy when it comes to HIPAA compliance.

HIPAA COMPLIANCE CAN BE A DAUNTING TASK

Over the years, as part of my regular engagements with medical practices, I began discussing HIPAA. It quickly dawned on me that practices wanted to be compliant, but for the most part they didn't know how or where to start. They didn't want to spend 'boat loads' of money for something that has no return on the investment. They thought that downloading some "fill in your name here" forms and getting online training were adequate. They mistakenly thought if their electronic medical records (EMR) system was compliant, they were okay. Some practices went so far as to assume if they changed their passwords regularly, all was well. One practice told me, "Our people know what not to say." This was the answer to my question, "What are you doing for a compliance program?"

I realized that what was necessary was to build a "culture of compliance." As you know, when developing a culture within a group there isn't a single "something" or a "silver bullet" to make it happen. The reality is that there are lots of "somethings" and the important thing is to have a strategic game plan to begin moving toward compliance. It's not a sprint, it's a marathon. It's a journey. You have to change the way people within your practice think about what they are doing and how they are doing it. You need to have all the information necessary to make educated decisions about where to start and what is "reasonable and appropriate" for your organization.

RAMIFICATIONS OF NOT BEING HIPAA COMPLIANT

Medical practices are stewards of patient's medical information. The patient is actually the owner of the information, the medical practice just happens to be holding it and utilizing it so they can deliver to the patient cohesive and proper medical care.

Unfortunately, ePHI is compromised on a daily basis throughout the nation. When this information falls into the hands of thieves, it is sold on the Internet and through other underground sources. What happens if someone steals your health insurance, Medicare or Medicaid information? They can make Doctor appointments, get medical tests, give birth, even have surgery all in your name. With this information unscrupulous people also steal your identity to commit other criminal acts such as credit card fraud.

If A Breach Occurs There Are Very Specific Regulations That Must Be Followed!

The U.S. Department Of Health and Human Services (HHS) states: "Following a breach of unsecured protected health information, covered entities must provide notification of the breach to affected individuals, the HHS Secretary, and the media in cases where the breach affects more than 500 individuals. Breaches affecting fewer than 500 individuals will be reported to the HHS Secretary on an annual basis." The regulations also require business associates of covered entities to notify the covered entity of breaches, at or by the business associate.

The final Rule moves HIPAA enforcement toward a penalty-based system with a tiered structure that ranges from $100 to $50,000 per violation with a $1.5 million cap per calendar year for multiple identical violations. Criminal penalties can be up to ten years of imprisonment. Willful neglect is at the top of the scale with the most severe penalties. HHS describes willful neglect as: "Conscious, intentional failure or reckless indifference to the obligation to comply with the administrative simplification provision violated."

STEPS A MEDICAL OFFICE MUST TAKE TO BECOME HIPAA COMPLIANT:

1. Review and Update HIPAA Policies and Procedures Manual.

This is a very important step. Many of the requirements have been updated and modified by the Omnibus Rule. You need to know what they are, how they have changed and document accordingly.

2. Choose a person (or two) to become the Privacy Officer(s) and the Security Officer(s).

HIPAA regulations state that you must formally designate a Privacy Officer and a Security Officer, these can be the same person.

A Privacy Officer is the official within a Covered Entity that is responsible for the development and implementation of the policies and procedures.

A Security Officer is the official who is responsible for the development and implementation of the policies and procedures required by the security rule.

3 Have a thorough risk assessment completed.

This assessment will evaluate risk and exposure from physical security within the practice to technology security to properly disposing of unneeded information, computers, etc. HIPAA compliance involves more than just your network.

Getting a proper risk assessment done is also one of the core objectives that must be completed before the practice can qualify for getting stimulus dollars to upgrade to Electronic Medical Records (EMR). In order for a practice to obtain Meaningful Use Dollars, a governmental subsidy program, there are fifteen core objectives they must meet and number fifteen on that list is a Proper Risk Analysis. The risk analysis has numerous steps that must be taken and certain criteria that must be met to qualify as a proper risk assessment.

4. Train your staff.

Effective employee training is essential, this cannot be stressed enough. In 2009 and 2010 the most common HIPAA breaches were theft of patient health information, unauthorized access to the data, human error, loss and improper disposal of patient records.

5. Update Business Associate Agreements (BAAs).

It is important to be sure they are consistent and pertinent. We too often see BAAs that are simply copied templates from an EMR vendor or other outside companies that are used for all other outside vendors.

One of the most important elements of the Omnibus regulation is the breach notification requirement. If you are a covered entity, it is your problem if a business associate has a breach, even though under the new rule they have a legal obligation to meet various HIPAA requirements. Your Business Associate Agreement should clearly state what the BA needs to do, rather than a catch-all "we agree to follow all applicable laws" although this may be compliant.

6. Update Notice Of Privacy Practices.

The Omnibus Rule makes some changes in how practices can use or disclose a patient's Protected Health Information (PHI). As a result, you have to include those changes in your Notice of Privacy Practices.

HAVING A COMPLIANCE PLAN DOESN'T MEAN YOU'RE COMPLIANT

Attention must also be given to the day-to-day details taking place within the medical practice. For example, employees writing their passwords on a sticky note and posting them on the back of their monitors, being never allowed to change their passwords or sharing their passwords with others around the office. These are not sound practices, and even more to the point, they are violations, since there is no way to track access by individuals to ePHI. There are many examples like this. HIPAA compliance means you are consistently evaluating your processes and the actions of your staff – in light of your designated policies and procedures.

A compliance program is a work-in-progress and must be revisited at least each year or when circumstances warrant. For example, on April 8, 2014, Microsoft will end support for the decade-old Windows XP. This means you will no longer receive updates, including security updates, for Windows XP from Microsoft. Support of Microsoft Office 2003 will also be ending on the same date.

Any computers with Windows XP after that date will be in violation of the regulation. In order to become compliant, the office will have to install and use a supported operating system and their Compliance Plan must be adjusted accordingly to reflect this change. Other technologies that affect compliance are: data backups, encryption, anti-virus software, firewall/router, smart phones, tablets, etc.

YOU NEED A TRUSTED TECHNOLOGY PROVIDER THAT SPECIALIZES IN MEDICAL PRACTICES

Medical practices have unique needs when it comes to technology. As a technology firm specializing in medical practices, our goal is to mitigate fear, uncertainty and doubt with respect to technology. Doctors and practice managers need a trusted technology advisor and a "go-to" person that has a thorough understanding of the overall landscape and not just a firm that is focused on fixing a problem when something breaks.

Does your technology provider fully understand the nuances of a medical practice? There is a unique set of equipment and applications that must be managed, monitored and maintained by professionals with specific expertise in the medical technology field. Doing things the wrong way can be very costly and disruptive to a medical practice. The managing of the technology in a medical practice is a specialty, and you should be dealing with professionals that have a wider and deeper knowledge of what happens in a medical practice and all the associated variables.

THE REAL PRICE OF TECHNOLOGY IN A MEDICAL PRACTICE

There are dollars that practices should be spending as a budgetary line item for technology. I have found if a practice is not spending an amount commensurate with their activity, number of employees and other measures, one of two things are happening – either someone is doing work and it isn't being considered and calculated as an IT expense or there are IT related issues within the practice.

One doctor called me recently to inquire about our Hassle Free IT MD service. I asked, "What made you call us now?" He replied, "I'm spending 20 hours a month dealing with issues related to my technology, there isn't anyone else here that can handle the day-to-day issues."

When is he doing that work? It can't be during the time he's seeing patients, so it has to be after hours or on the weekends. Some offices are not counting the time spent by their providers or other non-IT professionals that are trying to deal with technology issues when they could be doing something more profitable. What is the time worth of those medical professionals that are trying to deal with technology issues? What value does the practice put on their time?

In some cases, medical practices must feel the pain from not having the proper technology or not having the correct technology provider before they make the decision to invest in their technology. This happened with a medical practice that I visited recently. While I was there, the managing provider said to his practice manager, "We want to see if we can do business with this company. Give them whatever information they need so they can come up with a price for us." They had the usual issues and concerns not only with their computers and network, but also with their ability to communicate between offices using the telephones. Patients couldn't be transferred between offices, employees had trouble accessing records reliably, systems locked up etc., etc.

Surprisingly, the practice manager gave me the general ledger sheets for the practice. I've never had that happen before. On the ledger sheet I saw expenditures for telephone, computers, antivirus, etc. I quickly discovered they were spending twice as much as they should for telephone service and not nearly as much as they should for everything else. So I started to ask questions to see if I was missing something. The practice manager assured me that what I saw was the extent of their expenditures for technology and lamented about how much their communications cost each month.

As part of my assessment, I did an onsite visit to one of their busier offices. I went into the server room and was there for about two minutes when someone came into the room and asked, "What did you do?" They caught me by surprise and I quickly replied, "I didn't do anything. I am taking an inventory of your equipment." Another person walked by and stated, "Our server just went down." The second person said, "That's no big deal, it happens every day." She told me that for the last year or so they have been having problems daily. She went on to say, "Our network goes down and locks us out of our EMR system. Our IT people have given us multiple logins so when the network comes back up we can log back in. But, when we get blocked from the EMR system, we call one of the other offices. They make our appointments for us and look up the information we need." At that moment, I knew I had discovered the pain.

I went back to the practice manager with this information and she said she had no idea that was happening.

YOU GET WHAT YOU PAY FOR

Two old adages come to mind when I think of the value of technology services: "There's no such thing as a free lunch." and "You get what you pay for." I have seen time and time again, medical practices trying to cut corners to save a few dollars only to find that their shortcut attempts end up costing them thousands of dollars and sometimes they don't even know it. Technology should be viewed as an investment and not as an expense. It allows you to do your job in a more efficient manner, and in many cases, moves you closer to compliance by employing best practice technologies.

When technology is working right, it makes everyone's life much easier. Not only will your practice be more resourceful, but also you will undoubtedly notice an improvement in staff morale. No one likes to work with inept equipment or networks that are always crashing. Your investment in the proper technology and the appropriate technology provider will be an investment in your success.

About Peter

For over 27 years, Peter Verlezza has been the architect of technology solutions that make sense for medical practices, businesses and non-profits. His unique way of approaching challenges comes from a belief that it all starts with people.

In the early years, Peter worked at his family's deli and catering businesses where the foundation of exemplary customer service was instilled by his family. The value of serving has extended to his professional relationships with clients as well. Peter internally asks the question, "Is this in the best interest of the client?" while remembering the old saying, "You can't change what you have been handed only how you deal with it." He approaches both of these with a sense of humor, charisma and genuine care for others – it's become a way of life.

Many businesses are limited in their technological strengths, yet when they become a client of SMB Networks they immediately are included in the family style inner circle that has the ability to provide the strength necessary to transport the business to the intended goals. The deli days are long gone, but the overall interest for each client is still very much flourishing.

Peter designed and developed Hassle Free HIPAA™ – a complete HIPAA compliance program for Covered Entities, Business Associates and IT companies. He is an author of two other books, *Hassle Free IT – MD* and the Amazon Best-seller, *The Tech Multiplier.*

CHAPTER 17

BUSINESS APPLICATIONS:
KEY POINTS TO UNDERSTANDING THE HEART OF ANY SUCCESSFUL OPERATION

BY JUSTIN LENKEY

THE BASICS

They are truly the lifeblood of any business. They are designed to keep track of every aspect of a company's operation. They are business applications. Business applications refer to any software or set of computer programs that are used to increase and measure productivity and perform business functions accurately. The key concept to understand while discussing a line of business applications is that this software, in many cases, runs the business. When talking about the applications, the primary focus is on solving a business problem and usually not anything directly computer related. So if a company has a practice in the medical field, that organization would use software that manages patient billing and medical records, if in manufacturing and distribution, they might use ERP (Enterprise Resource Planning) or WMS (Warehouse Management Software) software.

These business problems can cost companies substantial amounts of money. As a result, business applications are designed and implemented to help reduce the cost of the problem and can even eliminate entire steps in a process. So when choosing the proper business applications, a company must make sure that their solutions will give the company a strategic advantage and help control the process while eliminating extraneous paperwork and manual labor. The goal is to use software that makes a business more productive and efficient, in order to help facilitate and create a competitive advantage with customers or, if in a health-related field, with patients.

IDENTIFYING KEY OBJECTIVES

When considering business applications, the discussion should center less on specific software and hardware and more around the bigger picture; what will create a competitive advantage for your company while creating a strong ROI and making your business run efficiently. The questions can be as simple as, "How can my business be more accurate and efficient in fulfilling customer's requirements?" For distribution companies, or in the medical field: "How can my company best fulfill the vendor-client compliance issue that has to be met?" Key objectives during this part of the decision should revolve around whether the solution being considered will work with how the business works today. Consider if the software balances the way the company fulfills orders, or will it necessitate a change in the way business runs in order to manage the application properly. After implementing new software, there might be six steps to complete the order process, whereas before there may have only been four steps. On first glance, this may be perceived as a loss of efficiency. However, the additional steps can gather data and provide greater operational detail that is valuable to shoring up the bottom line.

Sometimes it is difficult to see how using applications can reflect a shift from traditional approaches of doing business to a profitable, effective technological business solution. Consider a company that makes car parts. Traditionally, employees write down everything on paper – from orders to tallying how many parts they made. The company would use a handwritten piece of paper attached to the part to reflect that it was catalogued and then move on to the next step in the process, perhaps it was boxing and shipping the part, also using paper and pen. The process is slow and manually intensive, though comprehensive. This same company decides to integrate these processes by adding software. The user would scan a bar code and prints out everything that was once written by hand. The application system can keep track of how many parts are being produced per hour and exactly where items are in the system in real time. By embracing a technological method of doing business this company has become much more productive and cost effective.

The healthcare or even biomedical research fields can utilize this same model. Under the old system, the company takes a vial of blood for processing and attaches a piece of paper to the specimen. All the tests are run with that notation attached which has the propensity to be misplaced. In modern medical facilities, all specimens are bar coded. The computer prints out labels for each vial, and each step is captured electronically. The person collecting the sample scans the bar code and the lab personnel scans the sample again to ensure the test is completed on the correct vial.

No system is perfect. However, business applications are meant to be error proof. Their objective is to create an efficient, cost-effective business by tracking things that were unaccountable before.

INTEROPERABILITY

Interoperability is an important consideration when investigating various software packages. Each business has its own needs and specifications. If a law firm is looking for new software to help run their offices, they may want to be able to do things like keep track of calls to clients and record dictation. When selecting an application to run daily operations, it is important to contemplate the ability to add new functionality to enhance those applications already in operation. Essentially the firm wants to adopt an application that allows for expansion and modification since business conditions change all the time. It is important for software applications to be flexible to emerging programs and technologies.

Accounting packages are useful for many areas, but do not normally keep track of other issues such as customer service. These areas are still important to business operations, but are less quantifiable. In order to keep track of customer information, a business might consider adding a CRM (Customer Relationship Management) application, which will allow the company to track salespeople and customer interactions. In this example, the accounting package would have to be adaptable so that it could be enhanced as the business needs change.

USABILITY

Sometimes it's the little things in business that get on our nerves the most. I was working with a client recently whose employees had a very valid complaint. Apparently an application they were working with required them to go in and out of a single screen seven times in order to fulfill one customer order. Just to look up and work with other pieces of information. What a waste of time! This application was clearly not meeting their needs. It was completely unusable. Instead, we devised a way to change the software the system was running on so that employees only had to leave the main screen one time and had all the information at their fingertips simultaneously. Comparatively, the old software was designed inefficiently. Those seemingly tiny changes not only eliminated a slew of frustration, but the employees taking orders were now saving five to ten minutes with each customer. That customer order system deals with ten thousand orders a month; the time they saved with each customer amounted to a great deal of additional revenue.

"Usability" means "easy to use." It is making sure that the applications selected provide an organization with the most efficient ways necessary to complete the objective. In this case, it meant taking a customer order in the fewest necessary steps, with the greatest amount of error checking possible. Usability is not just about changing the way an application works in order to increase efficiency at a company. Sometimes the end user, and not simply the database, needs to be considered. For example, one company may need a software solution that utilizes pictures in order to help the person taking the order to describe the product to the customer as opposed to a text-based application. Graphics and illustrations may allow the end user to complete their business tasks with greater ease, therefore bringing greater success to the company.

Let's say a manufacturer has a bill that itemizes the materials used to create the finished product. Some software may list the items: say 12 washers and five screws, while more modern software – rather than just providing lists and textual information – will offer an illustration of the components and where those items are used. This helps the customer service representative understand the product better – allowing them to convey details more accurately to customers and to solve their problems in ways that would not be possible in a program written in text. For the business goals, the illustrations allow for greater usability.

BACKEND ARCHITECTURE

Making sure applications run on a database or operating system that is not proprietary is another consideration. Backend architecture refers to reliability, security and how the operating system integrates with functions like the web and mobility. For instance, it is easy to find someone to work on a SQL database, and that means there are thousands of IT Professionals who can make sure the system is functioning and backed up properly. But if a company uses a custom database, they have a much smaller talent pool to choose from. When selecting software, it is important to make sure a business uses platforms that are open and well supported.

An important consideration is the ease with which the system can be customized, as well as the cost involved, when deliberating on a solution that uses a Cloud-based backend. It is critical to ensure a solutions provider has a clear path to retrieve usable copies of data in the event that a business must change platforms or retrieve data. For example, a business decides that the current CRM software it uses no longer fits its needs and finds a better solution for their evolving infrastructure. Unfortunately, upon implementing the current CRM application, the company failed to consider proprietary policies. As a result they are not guaranteed their data will be provided to them in a usable format for migration. This can result in loss of revenue and require additional human capital to migrate to a new platform.

MOBILITY

With modern demands placed on business functions, technology now means availability. If an application needs to be used externally, software that allows multiple methods of accessing information is needed. A company must ensure that applications can function wherever they are needed. This equates to a desire for business applications to be mobile. In the past, lawyers working outside of the office may have used yellow pads to take dictation. Today they have the option of using tablet applications to do everything from taking notes to managing billing, which allows for greater flexibility.

Mobility is one of the great wonders of a modern, technological world; giving organizations the ability to take customer orders at the moment the sale occurs and noting it on the inventory list in real time, rather than writing it down and entering it in a system later. This immediacy lessens the possibility of transcription errors and allows for greater business profitability.

RETURN ON INVESTMENT (ROI)

When it comes to ROI, the big question for most businesses looking for the perfect software is, "How quickly can the investment be recouped?" For those on the fence, pondering whether it's worth it, consider this real world example. I have a client who works with automotive customers. They deal with hundreds of parts that are stored on warehouse shelves. Previously when orders came in, the employees took too much time to physically locate the parts. There was a great deal of downtime involved in finishing the task in this manner, but there was no other true way to track how much this was costing the business. My company came in and put a dollar value on the current business practices while removing the wasted downtime with a bar code driven, itemizing system that made everything very efficient. The economy was in a dip, but doing this allowed my client to process twice as many orders with half the employees. The cost of the software was quickly cancelled out by the gain in operation efficiency. A very quick return on investment also happened with a client that sells food products. Their previous system led to an abundance of spoilage with the occasional error of selling items with a diminished shelf life to customers. Within ninety days of starting to use the new software, the client made their investment back and created better and more controlled business practices.

GROWTH

As already stated, it is imperative that software will grow with your company. Therefore, when selecting or working with an application, it's important to consider one that can expand as your business does. Times change and it's important to have different ways to look at things. For example, a business starts a new venture with a client that will comprise 30 percent of their business. But this new client has compliance requirements that had never been a concern before. The business will start to examine whether or not there was existing software that could grow to meet these new challenges. Some company's fail to consider that simply adding more applications to the current database to make it compatible with the existing system is a viable option. In doing this, the company is able to keep the existing software in place and create software customizations so they can use it to take the required different approach with this huge new client. This solution can be the best possibility since it accommodates the client's business growth by allowing the applications to grow along with it.

VENDOR COMMITMENT

Finally, a word about vendor commitment. It's important that the organization which a business chooses to implement business application systems, is a partner that can visit their locations and have a true understanding of what goes into daily functions – whether that means managing patients, manufacturing and shipping parts or anything else. Not only should this vendor have a strong overview of the company, industry requirements and its specific technical needs, but the organization needs competency in both software AND hardware.

One of the main things an organization should look for is industry experience, making sure that the vendors working with your employees bring to the table a diverse background of relevant experience in your industry. It is important that the software vendor understands the relevant terminology and requirements related to business practices. A company cannot afford to allow someone to make crucial decisions for them without fully understanding the implications of how that relates to the industry. That organization should also have functional and technical familiarity with the company, understanding not only how to perform a transaction in the software but what happens after that occurs. After a company finds an IT professional they like, they should consult with other companies that have a similar business structure who have used that provider to make sure they are reputable and their work is exemplary. The most important thing to realize when considering IT vendors, is to view the IT professional not just as a supplier but as a partner – the future success of the organization could depend on it!

About Justin

Justin Lenkey helps his clients extend the functionality of their technology and fully maximizes their investments. He does this with the idea that technology does not have to be overly complicated to the consumer, and therefore, is dedicated to help his clients understand their technological investments in plain English. Over his career he has worked with a diverse range of clients in various environments including healthcare, food processing, petrochemical, manufacturing and transportation and logistics. All of Justin's clients are given personalized solutions that are created with industry-best practices in order to improve their business systems.

As an expert in Enterprise Resource Planning and warehouse management techniques and practices, Justin is able to improve operational efficiency and help his clients better serve their customers and stay competitive. He regularly offers continuing education events to his clients that are designed to enhance each user experience in the products they invest in. Ensuring that IT and business solutions produce solid results has never been more critical to the longevity and success of an organization. By focusing on proactive maintenance, security and infrastructure solutions and custom applications, Justin can collaborate with individual companies in order to ensure the success of their partnership.

Justin is Founder and Managing Partner of Argyle IT Solutions – a leading IT services provider that works in relationship with Fortune 1000 companies. Argyle focuses on increasing business productivity by managing and supporting both Hardware and Software while offering a single point of contact for any issue a company might have. Dedicated to being an extension of a company's IT team, Argyle continues to support and educate their clients beyond the scope of a traditional IT services provider. The customer must be successful in order for Argyle to consider their project successful.

CHAPTER 18

COMPLIANCE

BY RANDY SPANGLER

My company, MERIT Solutions, was founded in 1982. From day one, I have been involved with computers and with small to medium-sized businesses (SMBs). I have had a front row seat to the evolution of security in this sector and I deal every day with many of the security-related topics covered in this book – from employee monitoring and email filtering to backup, disaster recovery, business continuity, mobile computing and firewalls. Just as important as the "how" of the technical details of each of these topics, is the "why" of implementing these safeguards.

For small businesses and huge corporations alike, implementing security measures seems like it just makes good business sense, but sometimes good business sense is not enough to get people to "do the right thing." Sometimes people need a little incentive to take action, and in today's increasingly complex business climate, that incentive is taking the form of compliance requirements.

This is an interesting time to write a chapter on compliance. As this book goes to press, there is an almost epidemic distrust of just about anything from the government. Institutions that we once trusted to protect us seem complicit in gathering and organizing information heretofore assumed to be off-limits. Computer programs and massive data centers designed to operate health insurance marketplaces, run the FBI, modernize the air traffic control system and track immigrants are unreliable, decades behind their target date and billions of dollars over budget.

The idea of casting our votes in elections totally electronically seems ludicrous, yet we confidently spend billions of dollars every day using nothing more than plastic cards and a string of numbers.

At the same time, rules and regulations are in place with the force of law requiring businesses to meet specific standards.

In order to be compliant with these security rules, small business owners are asked to secure their data from harm, ensure availability and reliability of their data, write and implement meaningful policies and procedures, train their workforce, and meet nebulous specifications and requirements, all while trying to manage a profitable business.

Couple those requirements with the fact that if you fail to meet the spirit, if not the letter of the regulation, you may be subject to civil or criminal monetary penalties. You might be asking yourself, *why*? Why should you be compliant when the same agencies which require your compliance cannot meet it themselves? Why should you attempt to be compliant, especially now, when there are few small companies being audited? Why not just wait for the audit notification, then plead poverty... or ignorance... or both?

The answer is rather simple. If you strip away the technical jargon and the official language of law and regulations, most of the security measures just make good logical sense. After all, who wants their network or facility to be insecure? Would you want to be subjected to repeated attacks from cyber-warriors? Would you want malicious strangers picking through your confidential information and removing money from your bank account, or even worse, from your client's account? Remember this: no one is going to protect your business but you!

So, what if you did take a proactive stance toward security and you implemented safeguards such as improved firewalls, strong password policies and updated physical security? Would it be enough? Would your actions meet specific requirements of HIPAA if you are a medical practitioner or GLBA if you are a financial institution? How would you even know?

Enter *compliance*. In the modern business context, compliance is the state of being in alignment with relevant regulations, usually involving activities and physical means which are not part and parcel of a company's normal workflow. For instance, a business owner may have electronic locks throughout his property and he may have an installed security system, but being compliant with regulations might involve him performing daily security log reviews, submitting periodic reports, meeting certain rules pertaining to the length of the passcode needed to gain access to the property and having written company policies describing these rules.

Compliance requirements and the potential risk to a business if the regulations are not followed have been huge barriers to entry for new startups. Big businesses, many of whom actually help regulators write the regulations, stand to gain from this barrier by discouraging new competition. They have the deep pockets and the scale to comply with regulations and they have enough money to pay the fines if they get caught out of compliance.

All is not lost for SMBs, however. Like preparing tax returns, or writing contracts, you should not feel like you have to do this alone. Help is available and if done properly, your business will be more secure, your clients will be more protected and you, the stakeholder, will have one less thing to worry about.

How to proceed? Let's take a closer look at the health care industry. Even if you are not involved in the medical business (and you may be surprised to find out that you are), it is a microcosm of the state of compliance across many industries today.

THE GOVERNMENT FINALLY GETS CRACKIN' ON HIPAA – 17 YEARS LATER!

Americans who believe our government is more than a little slow on the uptake have some strong evidence for their viewpoint with the long and winding journey between writing the law, designing regulations and release of the final ruling of The Health Insurance Portability and Accountability Act (HIPAA) of 1996.

Generally when Congress passes a law, an agency is assigned to draft regulations to implement the law. Think of the law as *policy* and the regulations as *procedures*. These proposed regulations are posted in the Federal Register and are open for comment. After a 60-90 day time frame, the comments are reviewed, lobbyists are met with, updates are made and an interim rule is established which allows the law to be enforced. The interim rules may also be subject to review and comment. If it is a law that affects many or if the subject of the law is complex, this process can take a long time to complete.

With HIPAA, it was an astonishing 17 years between the time the law passed and the final ruling was adopted!

As you learned in a previous chapter, HIPAA is a large, multi-disciplinary, widely-encompassing law. For compliance purposes, we are primarily interested in <u>Title II, Subtitle F – Administrative Simplification</u> of HIPAA. No, that is not a typo, it is actually called *Administrative Simplification*. This section amended Title XI (42 U.S.C. 1301) by adding Part C. In Part C, Section 1173 of the amended law addresses "Standards for Information Transactions and Data Elements" and within this section it breaks down requirements for what is now known as the Privacy Rule and the Security Rule. Of the entirety of this 169-page law, less than one full page of text spawned what are commonly known as "HIPAA regulations."

In order to create the regulations, Congress actually tasked itself with creating these rules and it gave itself one year to do so. Failing that deadline, the task would fall to the Secretary of Health and Human Services (HHS). So, a year after the bill became law, HHS began working on the rules.

- The Privacy Rule was released first with an effective compliance date of April 14, 2003 with a one year extension for "small plans."
- The Final Rule on Security Standards was issued February 20, 2003. It had a compliance date of April 21, 2005 and a one year extension for "small plans."
- The Enforcement Rule was issued on February 16, 2006, establishing civil money penalties for HIPAA rule violations and establishing administrative procedures. However, few prosecutions for violations ever occurred.
- In 2009, Congress passed the American Recovery and

Reinvestment Act (ARRA), commonly known as "The Stimulus." Title XIII of that law was the Health Information Technology for Economic and Clinical Health (HITECH) Act. The HITECH rules modified HIPAA's privacy and security rules. It also extended these provisions to encompass business associates of covered entities and it imposed new breach notification requirements. Regulations associated with these new requirements were issued in late 2009.

- In July 2010, final modifications to the HIPAA privacy, security and enforcement rules mandated by the HITECH Act and certain other modifications to improve the rules were issued as a proposed rule. The release, review and modification process of this proposed rule culminated in the release of what is called the Omnibus Rule, but technically is the *final*, <u>Final</u> Rule (emphasis mine).

The Omnibus Rule was issued January 25, 2013 with an Effective date of March 26, 2013 and a Compliance date of September 23, 2013. This represents a total of 17 years between the time the original HIPAA legislation was passed into law and the date which the compliance really, *really* will begin to be enforced. During the interim period between passage of the previous Final Rules and the September 2013 Compliance date, most practices (doctors, dentists and other medical offices) were focused on the privacy side of the law and not the security side.

With the privacy rules addressing primarily administrative procedures, adopting the requirements of the Privacy Rule was somewhat familiar territory for most practices. Most, for instance, made sure that patients signing in at the front desk couldn't see other people's names who had signed in above them, while computer and electronic security—things like preventing people from hacking into their system or making sure computers have strong passwords—went largely ignored. Since it was rarely enforced through audit, the Security Rule, which had no natural constituency within most smaller practices, laid dormant. Dormant, that is, until the release of the Omnibus Rule and the specter of actual enforcement.

September 23, 2013 was D-Day for the HIPAA requirements. Although the rules had been in effect since 2005, health care professionals had no more excuses. If they willfully neglected the rules, they could be hit with stiff fines – which could amount to $1.5 million dollars for each infraction, even for small businesses!

HOW DO WE GET THERE FROM HERE?

The reason I described the torturous process that culminated in the release of the Final Rule was to underscore the point that few mortals would be able to follow this process and stay within the law, even if they tried. Professional associations, especially those who lobby on behalf of their members, can help and in the case of HIPAA, they did a good job with the Privacy Rule. Because the Security Rule is so technical and vague, it was largely ignored.

With the passage of the HITECH law and the tens of thousands of dollars in incentive money on the table, many providers jumped onboard the Electronic Health Records (EHR) bandwagon. In order to actually receive the cash, providers had to 'attest' to achieving three stages of Meaningful Use. For example, Stage One – Core Objective 15 for Eligible Professionals is to "Protect electronic health information." This is a requirement to conduct a security risk analysis per 45 CFR 164.308 (a)(1), which is part of the HIPAA regulation. Now, it suddenly became important to look at the security portion of HIPAA, especially in light of the fact that failure to meet <u>every</u> Core Objective could cause the incentive money to be revoked.

As an IT managed service provider, companies pay me to oversee the tech side of their business and I have clients who practice medicine. HIPAA requires that any person (business associate – BA) who deals with a health-related company (covered entity - CE) and has contact with protected health information (PHI), needs to meet the same compliance standards as the CE. After becoming aware of the rules, *I suddenly realized that this meant me!* I was in the military for many years during which I developed an understanding of "government speak" – but these rules and regulations were hard to comprehend. I had to figure it all out.

If I, with my background in computer security, was having difficulty with the Security Rule, how could my clients be expected to comply? I knew that I would have to help them and the best way to help would be to take the steps to make my company compliant.

SO WHAT DOES IT TAKE TO BECOME COMPLIANT?

It became apparent rather quickly that security compliance involves a few defined steps:

- Conduct a security risk assessment.
- Identify risk factors based upon the risk assessment.
- Develop a plan to remediate the shortcomings.
- Create security policies and the procedures to implement them.
- Train all of the company's staff on security policy and awareness.
- Update documents as progress is made.
- Review, at least annually, or as changes occur.
- Repeat, because security compliance is a journey, not a destination.

Unfortunately, the regulations provide no real guidance on how to accomplish these steps, nor do they let you know if your process is correct.

Fortunately, there is guidance if you know where to look.

HELP FROM THE SAME FOLKS WHO MAKE SURE THE BALL DROPS IN TIMES SQUARE PRECISELY AT MIDNIGHT ON NEW YEAR'S EVE

You may not have heard of NIST, the National Institute of Standards and Technology, but they are tasked with providing national standards for inches, ounces, gallons, barrels and other measurements, including time. They make sure that when the Mayor of New York City pushes the button to drop the crystal ball on New Year's Eve, it reaches bottom precisely at midnight. But NIST works the rest of the year, too.

Government agencies have their own compliance standards, defined by the Federal Information Security Management Act of 2002 (FISMA). NIST was tasked with setting security standards for the implementation of FISMA. Some of these federal agencies and departments also fall under HIPAA. NIST was then tasked to refine the security standards to also meet HIPAA requirements. The result of this effort is the NIST Special Publication 800-66 Rev 1 entitled "An Introductory Resource Guide for Implementing the HIPAA Security Rule." This publication, along with NIST SP 800-53 "Recommended Security Controls for Federal Information Systems and Organizations" provide the foundation for any serious compliance regime.

Though voluntary for non-governmental entities, NIST's publications have become the *de facto* global security standard. HHS's Office for Civil Rights (OCR) is responsible for providing annual guidance on the provisions in the HIPAA Security Rule. OCR has stated that meeting NIST standards are sufficient for HIPAA compliance. In other words, if you base the fundamentals of your compliance on NIST, you should not have to wonder if you are on the right track.

While I have focused on HIPAA compliance, other government security compliance regulations, which may affect SMB such as the GLBA/FTC Safeguards Rule and Sarbanes-Oxley (SOX), base their standards on the same NIST publications. The exception is PCI-DSS which is a private standard designed by the Payment Card Industry. Its rather stringent requirements are outside the scope of this chapter.

LET'S GET STARTED ON THE ROAD TO COMPLIANCE

Nothing about compliance is simple if done properly. In the beginning, I found it overwhelming trying to understand the nuances and fine details of compliance regulations and how to help my clients best navigate these waters. Clients who need to focus on building their practices or businesses while serving their patients or customers won't always have the time to set aside to figure out how to comply with the law. Fortunately, most compliance regimes are like HIPAA; they are quite flexible and allow you to address requirements over a timeline after you complete your required items. Others like PCI DSS are pretty much "check YES in every box or you fail." So, there are different philosophies based on which compliance regulations a business is required to meet.

I have come up with a few safeguards you can start using today to help your IT systems become more secure, put you in a security frame of mind and get you started on the road to compliance:

1) <u>Encrypt your laptops:</u> Even if you have a strong password on your laptop, thieves can take the hard drive out, mount it in their PC, and all your data and information is theirs for the taking. But, if your drive is encrypted, they cannot access anything. The loss isn't even

considered a breach. This is something your IT pro can do for you right now. One of the best ways to achieve this is a free software package called TrueCrypt (truecrypt.org).

2) <u>Affiliate with the association that oversees your industry:</u> The people who run those associations make it their business to help their members understand regulations, and are dedicated to keeping everyone informed about changes to relevant laws. A few examples would be: for car dealers, the National Automobile Dealers Association; for physicians, the American Medical Association; and for credit unions, the Credit Union National Association.

3) <u>Invest in cyber-insurance:</u> This can cover you for a lot of different security breaches and legal matters. For instance, if someone at your company blogs or Tweets something inappropriate and it comes back to harm your business, cyber-insurance can help cover the resulting damages. If you lose a laptop containing thousands of Social Security and credit card numbers, it can help you cover the mitigation expense. Cyber-insurance policy coverage varies greatly, so check with your insurance broker. (Some policies now require you to have certain security safeguards in place, to reduce risk.)

4) <u>Protect your smartphone:</u> Over 1.6 million smartphones were stolen last year. If you don't have a passcode on your device, <u>create</u> <u>one</u>! You could have health information related to your practice on your phone or information containing Social Security numbers or info on a tax audit in a Dropbox folder, text or email message. If you have a company-owned phone or if it's your phone with company data on it, you have a responsibility for that data. Protect it!

5) <u>Do not text or email personally identifiable information (PII):</u> Text messages and most email are NOT secure. It doesn't matter if the message is doctor to doctor or CPA to attorney, the transport and storage is not secure, so **don't do it!**

Now that you have a better understanding of what is involved with compliance, when someone offers you a simple, cheap or easy compliance package, don't just walk away from it... *RUN!* Like getting in shape, compliance takes effort and commitment, and the task is never totally complete, but with help from a competent IT professional your business or practice will be better for the effort – whether you get audited or not.

About Randy

From the age of 10, Randy knew he was destined to run his own business. After a promising career in lawn management was cut short by a faulty mower, he had several full and part time jobs before joining the Navy at age 17. Gaining real-world knowledge and experience in electronics, Randy developed several groundbreaking programs for the Navy after buying his own Apple II computer in 1977.

With a business partner, Randy started Micro-Enhancements in 1982, specializing in Apple computers and accessories. After leaving active duty in 1983, his first retail store was opened and quickly transitioned from Apple through CP/M, PC-DOS and MS-DOS into the world of IBM-PC compatibles. Throughout the 1990s, with as many as three stores open at once, a lot of computer equipment was sold which meant a lot of them needed repairs. Service was a big part of the business. Networks soon became affordable for small businesses and Randy became the lead installer of LanTastic, Novell, Windows for Workgroups and Windows NT LANs.

Around the time the Internet became relevant, he bought out his partner and renamed his business MERIT Solutions, reflecting the shift from microcomputers to computer-based solutions. MERIT Solutions was one of the first companies to begin implementing Microsoft's Small Business Server suite and hundreds of these networks were rolled out over 16 years, enabling local businesses to have an enterprise-level IT solution at an affordable price.

Randy retired from the U. S. Naval Reserve in 2003 as a Master Chief Petty Officer, spending most of his military career as a policy and security specialist.

In 2005, he pivoted and transitioned his company from retail to a managed-service provider. Investing heavily in technology, MERIT Solutions became an early adopter of the monthly flat-rate support model and leveraged Internet accessibility to provide support to hundreds and then thousands of endpoints both locally and nationally.

Recognizing the critical importance of computer and network security, he is now working to blend the increasing need for compliance with the proven popularity of managed services to provide a Compliance-as-a-Service offering.

Randy holds several Microsoft certifications. He is a Microsoft Partner and is currently a member of the Kaseya Customer Advisory Council. He lives in Norfolk, VA with his wife Nancy and their three golden retrievers. Learn more about Randy and MERIT Solutions at: www.meritsolutons.net or follow them at: www.facebook.com/meritsolutions and www.twitter.com/meritsolutions.

CHAPTER 19

MOBILE COMPUTING

BY ROBERT ZEHNDER

While mobile computing has seen a significant upsurge recently, I find that most organizations are deploying mobile computing solutions without the proper focus. Mobile computing should not be confused with cloud computing because there are distinct differences between the two. Since I have offices in different states, I do a great deal of traveling and a great deal of my work is completed through the mobile computing process. So, not only do I help my clients develop their mobile computing strategy, I literally live by the very strategies I help them develop for their businesses.

Mobile computing is on the rise because more and more people are working remotely or outside an office location. The information presented in this chapter will highlight the differences between Mobile Computing and cloud computing. I will also provide three essential components to assist you in creating your own enterprise mobility strategy.

WHAT IS MOBILE COMPUTING?

Mobile computing is the act of using a computer while traveling from place to place without the need of a continuous office network connection. Whereas, cloud computing is using systems that are sourced from the Internet or a centralized location rather than on your own machine or mobile device. One of the distinguishing characteristics of mobile computing is its independence from a network connection. It gives us the ability to work and do our job effectively by working remotely, away from an office, away from an Internet connection, and away from any corporate network. It should be understood that at some point those practicing mobile computing will have to connect to a network to upload their information and work they have completed from their mobile device. But, through mobile computing, the lack of a network or Internet connection doesn't impede the work that needs to be done. A couple of examples may be beneficial to better understand this concept.

EXAMPLES OF MOBILE COMPUTING

The Retail Distributor

About 10 years ago, when dial-up modems were still common in corporate networks, we worked with a company who had about 150 representatives nationwide delivering their product to a variety of retail outlets. During the fulfillment of their responsibilities, these representatives would put check marks on a piece of paper to monitor their deliveries and the in-store inventory. Then they would return to an office at the end of the day to tally all the data they collected on the pieces of paper they had for that given day. That data would then be entered into the company's information system.

Realizing the inefficiency of this archaic process, working with the company, we put a nine-inch tablet in the hand of every representative to accomplish the same routine task. They weren't connected to the Internet or to a network of any kind. The tablets were used for data gathering as a replacement to the pieces of paper they were dealing with on a daily basis. The application installed on the tablet enabled them to not only count what they delivered, but also allowed them to maintain an inventory of their product. When they returned to the office or arrived home at the end of the day they would plug their tablet into a network connection or use the modem to dial into the corporate network, hit one button, and all the information they collected that day would synchronize to the central system enabling all their data to be accurately tallied. Not only did this improve operations, but it also automated their invoicing. All the work on the tablet was done off-line without any network connection. Further upgrades to the application also allowed for the electronic signature and capture of the deliveries by the retail outlet personnel. It was pure mobile computing.

The Company with 100 Technicians Nationwide

Another company we worked with in the machining and aerospace industry had approximately 200 employees with more than 100 technicians. They were a service company who sent technicians onsite to their customers' locations to service or repair equipment. The company has six offices in various parts of the country and the technicians routinely go to a variety of companies in every state. To help them become more efficient, about four years ago we deployed brand new computers throughout their company, but we also deployed a mobile application for their technicians that integrated into their central Microsoft Dynamics Application. The mobile application allowed the technicians offline access to view the service record, update time and service details and record expenses for the visit. Enterprise mobility solutions always integrate into the central corporate application, but allow for the offline use of the application.

In this situation, the application was deployed onto each technician's local computer, and allowed them to synchronize the service record to the centralized Microsoft Dynamics Application. Some government agencies and companies do not allow outside vendors to be connected to their network. Obviously there is protected and proprietary data that many companies do not want to place in a position of vulnerability by having one of their vendors connecting to their network. In some cases, you even have to prove that you have a laptop that does not have wireless capability or you will not be able to enter their facility.

We developed a solution for them that can be fully utilized offline, but everyone was also supplied with a cellular modem or air card. About half the time, when they are working they are on the cellular network and had a secure VPN connection enabling them to connect with their home office network. However, all of the data was entered offline and then synchronized to the home office network.

The Mortgage Firm

Most mortgage brokers have their customers come into a centralized office where they work to complete all the necessary paperwork when applying for a mortgage. One of our mortgage firm clients has a centralized office, but most of their mortgage brokers work from home. Their business concept was to be more accessible to potential customers that needed their mortgage service. The solution we helped them develop was to give each mortgage broker a laptop computer with the mortgage application loaded onto the laptop. The broker would then go to the home of a potential customer or meet them at another convenient location. All the needed information would be typed into the application on the laptop. The applicant could even sign the application through an electronic device that was connected to the mortgage broker's laptop. Again, all this could be done in the convenience of the applicant's own home. The application would then be sent to the main office via a secure VPN and synced with the company's network. The staff at the main office would then process the application through the designated underwriting process.

HOW DO WE MAKE IT WORK?

Through the examples above you can see that the process is straightforward and it can bring a lot of efficiencies to work being done outside a traditional work environment. Yet, there are many, many details that must be considered and implemented to make this process effective.

What work can we do remotely? What applications should we use? How do we make the applications work? How do we include the security? How do we make the connections? How do we make all these things work together? How can the application be used? Can we resolve multiple issues with the same application? As you can see, the questions can go on and on. But, the basics of effective mobile computing come down to these three essential components: *Applications, Security*, and *Connectivity*. These items will be the framework to enable you to develop an effective and efficient enterprise mobility strategy.

I. Applications
The first step in mobile computing is determining the application that will make your business more efficient and drive greater profitability. If you have a particular problem you are trying to solve, there is probably an application that already exists to help you resolve the problem. Often these applications need to be adjusted for your particular use. However, it is very likely the solution already exists.

The primary component for an enterprise mobile strategy is to ensure the application installed on mobile devices can integrate into the central office application. Having an offline application that is an extension of the central office application is critical to the success of Mobile Computing. It doesn't make sense to enter data into a mobile application on a laptop, for example, then have to re-enter that data into another system. You will want to make sure your applications are integrated into the central system so that you only have to enter the data once.

Secondly, with the proliferation of tablet computers, some applications can be installed on non-Windows computers such as iPad, Android and other tablet computers. Your professional IT provider can help you find the application that will help you, as well as take the lead in implementing the application to maximize its efficiency.

II. Security

Once the application is determined, proper security measures must be implemented. This is a subject that can't be stressed enough. In today's technology environment, security is of utmost importance. In some industries there are extremely strict guidelines and regulations that govern the security related to the data collected and stored on your electronic devices. In some business verticals, such as healthcare, there are extensive fines and even imprisonment penalties for improperly securing data. It is virtually impossible for a business owner to stay abreast of every nuance related to these regulations. That's why it is extremely important to find a reputable, certified and professional technology provider to assist you in this all-important process.

When you are connecting back to your central office from your mobile device you need a good quality business class firewall with a secure VPN connection allowing you to secure the connection between your mobile device and the central network. Certain firewalls provide an 'always on' VPN connection. This type of VPN connection will ensure that the connection from mobile devices is always secure and encrypted while the mobile device is outside of the central office network.

Install encryption software onto laptop hard drives or utilize Self-Encrypting Drives, SED, for all corporate laptops. Encrypting the data on the hard drive of mobile devices is essential. This will assure the protection of your information if your mobile device was stolen. A tablet also needs to be encrypted and protected in the same way. Antivirus and antispyware must also be on each mobile device as part of your security measures. Also, make sure your mobile applications prompt for a username and password before use. Taking these steps may literally save your business one day.

Some businesses are migrating toward a "Bring Your Own Device" (BYOD) concept. In this scenario, the employee uses their own mobile device and the employer loads their application to the employee's device. The employee is responsible for the maintenance of his or her own device. The benefit to the company is that they can save money on the purchase of devices. If you are a BYOD company, the same security must be placed on a BYOD as on a company-owned device.

III. Connectivity

A quality Internet connection and Quality of Service (QoS) are very important to mobile devices. Certain traffic requires more priority than other traffic. For example, if I'm a mortgage broker and I'm using my mortgage application and talking on the phone at the same time, my phone call should have a better QoS than the mortgage application. If it takes my mortgage application 10 seconds instead of 5 seconds to load, it doesn't really matter. But if my phone call starts to break up, then that is unacceptable and could interfere with my ability to effectively conduct my business.

Mobile connectivity is constantly improving. Not very long ago, the best way to connect a laptop to the network was through the utilization of a 56K dial-in modem. Now we have 4G Cellular Modems or Wireless Wide Area Network (WWAN) built into laptops and tablets. Technology has taken us beyond the need for an external air card for connectivity. The devices with the built in 4G also enable a better quality connection.

At some point you will have to connect to the Internet to upload your data to your office network. So you will also want to make sure you have a quality Internet connection. It's interesting to find that most central offices do not have in place a Service Level Agreement (SLA) with their Internet provider. Without an SLA, if their Internet service has poor quality or goes down for some reason, the Internet provider is not obligated to have it restored in a specific period of time. An SLA is an agreement with the Internet Service Provider that says if their service fails or performs poorly, they will have it restored within a designated period of time. Having a guarantee of a quality Internet connection as part of an SLA is very important. For example, an Internet Service Provider may tell you that you have a 75 megabit connection, but that may be only when you're downloading data into the central office network. It may only be 15 megabits when you're uploading. That means, if you have a mobile device and you are trying to retrieve information from the central office network, your connection speed is going to be significantly slower. When you are establishing your framework for mobile computing, you want to make sure your connection is always going to be the same whether you are downloading or uploading.

You have to ask for an SLA that meets your standards. When you call an Internet Service Provider to establish a business class connection, you must ask them what type of connection they have **with** a Service Level Agreement. Typically, they will not bring up the SLA unless they are asked about it. You need to determine if an SLA is important to your business. Some businesses can't justify the extra cost that comes with an SLA and they feel they can continue offline for a reasonable amount of time without significant interruption to their business or their revenue stream. Other businesses can't afford to have any downtime at all, and will want to make sure they have an SLA that will meet their business needs.

The other option would be to establish two Internet connections through two different providers. It is very unlikely that both services would be down at the same time, thus ensuring you will always have a quality Internet connection.

MAKE MOBILE COMPUTING WORK FOR YOU

It doesn't matter if you are a company of 10 people or 1,000 people. Mobile computing can be beneficial to your business. By consulting with an experienced and qualified IT provider to develop an enterprise mobility strategy based on the three essential components outlined in this chapter, you can potentially realize an increase in productivity, efficiency and bottom line revenue for your business. Mobile Computing is definitely on the rise. I encourage you to carefully explore your options in this rapidly expanding environment and take advantage of the latest technologies available to give your business the greatest competitive advantage.

About Robert

A successful entrepreneur for the past fourteen years, Robert Zehnder has helped companies worldwide achieve their business goals through education and the use of technology. Robert's passion for technology and talent for translating *techno geek speak* into easy-to-understand English for executives and business owners led him to found Hodgson Consulting & Solutions, a technology-consulting firm headquartered in Chicago, IL.

In 2005, Robert realized a shift in the market and through research discovered that many companies were being overcharged and underserviced for technology services. In response, he then decided to create the Peace of Mind Business Solutions, a highly successful predictable pricing model for Information Technology Services.

Robert is a recognized authority in virtualization solutions. He has been honored consistently for his strategic role in developing certification exams for Citrix Systems. He has implemented global Microsoft Enterprise Server Solutions for companies systems throughout Asia Pacific, Europe and North America. He continues to design and implement internal network infrastructures and multi-layer security solutions for companies throughout North America.

Robert currently has over 20 Industry Recognized Certifications and is an in-demand speaker on the topics of Network Security, Virtualization, Mobile and Cloud Computing.

Robert joined the Boy Scouts of America as a Boy Scout at age 11 and through hard work and diligence he became an Eagle Scout when he was seventeen. Robert has lived his life and run his business based on the values he learned as a Boy Scout. Robert is currently an awarded and recognized Cub Scout leader in his community.

CHAPTER 20

UNDERSTANDING MULTI-SITE NETWORK SOLUTIONS AND THE BENEFITS OF PUBLIC AND PRIVATE NETWORK CONNECTIONS

BY ROBERT BOLES

DEFINING WIDE AREA NETWORKS

A more popular term for the concept of Multi-site Network is Wide Area Network (WAN), which is one that covers a broad area using private or public network transports. It can be any telecommunications network that links across regional, national or global boundaries, which businesses use to share data among employees, clients, partners and suppliers in different geographical locations. WANs allow everyone to effectively carry on their daily work regardless of location or distance. The Internet itself can be described as a WAN, though typically the term WAN is used to describe multi-site connectivity for business purposes.

So how does it work on a day-to-day basis? Let's say we're in our office in San Francisco, and the company has another office in Chicago,

New York, London, or really anywhere. We need to access our servers but obviously there's no physical Ethernet cable to run across the country. So we plug our two networks together using either a private network, or IP VPN (Internet Protocol Virtual Private Network) via the public Internet with encrypted tunnels. A widely adopted example of a private network is what we call MPLS, or Multi-Protocol Label Switching. With MPLS, we can securely connect our local resources globally as required to support the business. There are different design and operational considerations for IP VPN and MPLS, and the most demanding networks will include both.

For many, the most cost effective means to facilitate WAN connectivity is via the public Internet, using IPsec/VPN with encryption. IPsec is an IP security standard that allows multi-vendor products to "speak" the same language. Secure connectivity can happen over any Internet connection, including DSL and Cable, which offer high bandwidth at lower cost, to dedicated lines like T1 or EoC (Ethernet over Copper), which provide greater reliability and expedient support. The IPsec standard is connectivity agnostic, allowing secure connectivity between peers over nearly any Internet connection. Private WAN are delivered via leased, or dedicated lines and are more expensive, though provide greater predictability, flexibility, and reliability. An example of predictability is if you are utilizing VoIP. With private connectivity, we can shape the traffic to prioritize the VoIP, resulting in more consistent overall call quality. With public Internet, we can tune and prioritize VoIP on the local network, though once it leaves it is "best effort" over the unpredictable Internet.

BREAKING DOWN PUBLIC VS. PRIVATE INTERNET

Those are the nuts and bolts of connectivity, but we can simplify things this way. The public Internet is essentially all these networks from Tier 1 (Global) providers like Level 3, AboveNet, and Savvis, to Tier 2 (Regional) providers such as Telepacific, and Tier 3 (Local) providers such as arbuckle.co – essentially anyone who provides data. The term "Cloud" has its origin in describing these separate yet interconnected networks. When you go out to the Internet, say onto Yahoo, you're basically going out to a server that lives somewhere in the cloud and when you get your Yahoo email, you're going to that server to get it. Your bank's website may be on yet other servers – but all are part of the public Internet or public cloud.

If you have public Internet that you use for business, you are connected to an untrusted space and should be protected behind a firewall. With a router, firewall, or VPN software between two or more locations, you create secure tunnels using encryption connecting all the sites together. Visualize your location scrambling the data, sending it out through the tunnel and there's a high tech secret decoder ring on the receiving end that makes sense of it only to the person who receives it. Here's the rub, though: while using the public Internet for business can be a little more cost effective, it's less predictable – which is saying, "less reliable."

When I say my company has a private network, I'm talking about an internal network that only authorized users from my company can see. My users in Chicago can traverse this private network and access my server internally that will give them information about our business – say, our calendar, training resources, whatever company information is available. Those connecting privately all have their own dedicated connections between offices. The office in Boston will have a private connection mapped through their service provider infrastructure to any other office location via any number of private lines: MPLS, VPLS (Virtual Private LAN Service), Frame-Relay and Metro Ethernet. Those are all examples of private connectivity. It's all internal, trusted traffic. If you have this, you're probably going to use it only for business because with a private connection, there's no way to get onto Yahoo, CNN or eBay.

THE MICHAEL JACKSON INTERNET CRASH – AND COST

One great benefit to using a private Internet is having more control over the particulars of the connection so as to avoid slow responses and crashes. Remember the intense public curiosity when Michael Jackson passed away? During his services, so many people were trying to stream the event online that it slowed the Internet down to a crawl on the West Coast. Likewise, using public Internet for your mission critical applications could leave you susceptible to unpredictable patterns or surges.

Let's use traffic as another example. The MJ funeral-streaming breakdown is the equivalent of the 405/101 interchange in Los Angeles (one of the busiest in the country) at 9 a.m. on a weekday. Too much traffic slows things down because too many people are trying to use the same lane at the same time. With public Internet, you kind of get what you get, and 90-95 percent of the time, maybe there's no issue. But when I talk to clients, I always warn, "It will always be an issue when it's least convenient for you."

Private connectivity costs more but provides greater flexibility to utilize it how you want. Plus it's higher quality, which always costs more but in the end means it's more predictable, more reliable and provides better service. My company spends a lot of time educating clients about the benefits and drawbacks of each option, and considering which is going to be more appropriate for each business. Networks are like people, no two are exactly alike, and the individual components and business requirements define the solution.

The MJ case is an extreme circumstance, but its impact cannot be overlooked.

PERCEIVED COST VS REAL COST

Cost is always a huge part of deciding which WAN connectivity option to invest in, but what you pay the carrier may not reflect the true cost. Depending on your type of business, your tolerance for down time and poor performance will dictate the type of connectivity you need. If you're okay with occasional down times and unpredictable performance, public Internet via DSL or cable is a very cost effective option coupled with IPSec VPN. If you have latency sensitive apps like VoIP (Voice Over Internet Protocol), or video, then dedicated Internet with IPSec VPN will provide a more reliable, predictable option. But if you have low or no tolerance for down time or unpredictable connectivity, private line will provide the highest level of predictability and performance. I have retail clients who run Point of Sale apps, and for them IPSec VPN over DSL/Cable is often sufficient. But for financial clients where uptime literally is money, they're using MPLS and resilient connectivity that provides maximum uptime.

Another thought to consider in relation with downtime due to lower cost Internet connections: losing sales in the retail environment. One client felt when he launched his business that it would be cost effective to have low cost connectivity at the stores. One day, his DSL went out while a clerk was waiting on a customer who wanted to ring something up. That person got frustrated and left the store without making a purchase – and that unpleasant shopping experience leads to this customer possibly never visiting the store again. In general, these kinds of things can affect employee morale, especially among those who work on commission. When these things happen, any perceived cost-saving just went out the window.

This particular client experienced several of those moments that were detrimental to business and ultimately transitioned to dedicated Internet connectivity. As a result, uptime increased to over 99%, making downtime a non-issue, though still lower cost than private line. Business owners who make the switch to dedicated private connectivity like MPLS essentially have the equivalent of a private highway between all their sites. They can prioritize traffic based on applications, giving VoIP the "Carpool Lane" while shaping the other data streams to support their own application needs. It's a matter of Quality of Service, or QoS. On public links, there is no QoS, but in the private network you can control the data from end to end, from L.A. to Boston to Orlando! Once we understand our clients' business, we can make recommendations as to what will best suit their needs.

TEN QUESTIONS: DETERMINING WHICH SYSTEM IS RIGHT FOR YOU

When I'm working with a new client and trying to determine the best way to approach his or her business' Wide Area Network needs, I ask the following questions:

- What are you trying to accomplish? This means getting the details about your business environment that help companies like ours design the right infrastructure. I cannot stress enough how critical it is to really understand your business needs, and how you leverage the network.

- What are the business applications requiring WAN connectivity? It's an extension of the first question. You always want to be clear on the apps because they all behave differently. As we put a solution together for a client, we want to uncover and remediate potential issues before they become issues. QuickBooks, for instance, will not work over WAN. Understanding client applications up front will save everyone headaches in the back.

- What is your voice solution? Is Voice Over IP currently in place or on the technology roadmap? What about video and/or Unified Communications?

- How many locations do you have, and where are they? City, address, zip code and phone number. This information helps us pre-qualify the location and assess the connectivity options in advance, to see what carrier offerings are available.

- Are your resources in a Carrier Data Center (Colocation) or in-house Data Center? Are there servers that deliver content to your users at your headquarters or a different location?

- What kind of existing connectivity is available at the sites?

- Are there existing assets which are serviceable? Meaning, is there existing hardware and network appliances like a router, switch, or firewall which can be leveraged as part of solution?

- This is one we covered earlier and it bears repeating: What is *your* tolerance level for downtime?

- Finally, what are clients' in-house management capabilities? This helps us understand where assistance will be valuable and how to craft a support solution.

CHOOSING THE RIGHT IT PERSON
FOR YOUR CONNECTIVITY NEEDS

Many businesses will have an in-house IT person who helps maintain their servers and offers helpdesk support. But when it comes to their networks, they will often rely on the carrier to provide the management and administration of their routers and MPLS. The challenge is that when you call your carrier with a problem, most times they will tell you everything is good from the carrier perspective, so the problem must be on your side. Then you get frustrated and finally finds a company specializing in telecommunications protocol, whose techs can look at your problem at a core level and remediate the issue. Having resources in-house full time is not cost effective, because in order to support a system like this it could take up to four full time people to provide 24/7 service. But when you partner with high-end network expertise (aka "Network Experts"), those people can look at all the data and identify where the issue is and provide granular protocol insight to solve your problem. So when we ask you what your in-house management capabilities are, we only ask that to gauge the appropriate level of support you need.

ELEMENTS OF CONNECTIVITY DESIGN

Companies like BLOKWORX manage hundreds of networks. I personally have designed managed network solutions for Fortune 50 companies and mom/pop regional organic food markets. Working in so many different environments, we are able to leverage our experience across our client base for the collective benefit of all current and future clients. This forms the basis of our design, integration, and management work that we provide for businesses like yours. The main task is to save hard-working business owners from wasting their time and money with systems and tools they don't need. The information we collect in the pre-design phase (the questions above) helps us put together an actual design featuring the following elements: ISP(s), CPE – router/switch/firewall/WAP, Layer 3 Protocol (dynamically routing traffic to facilitate redundancy), VLAN's/QoS, computing resources, Phones, Power, Subnet Consistency and Requirements for premise gear.

Although systems are customized based on your specific business needs, there are certain standards regarding the environment where the system is placed. Say a construction client wants to put in a router in a main work area. It might get covered in sawdust, which would damage it. So the systems must be in a temperature, dust and moisture-controlled room where the environmental specs are designed to house electronic appliances.

WHAT HAPPENS NEXT

Once the design of your system is complete, an integration plan is put together with the same level of detail addressing how the project will be completed, including ordering the equipment, staging, implementation, and acceptance criteria. Upon acceptance, the network moves to management and monitoring. Our NOC (Network Operations Center) has the ability to remotely access devices for administration and management, providing the day-to-day network infrastructure support enabling your in-house team to focus on taking care of your users. It all starts with up/down monitoring of devices (where our system alerts you via our NOC about a router or other device that goes offline, and we proactively work on getting it back up). Monthly performance reviews keep the teams on the same page. Backing up configurations, optimizing links, greater uptime are all components, but a BIG factor you should consider is: this service offering INCLUDES an ISP integrity check, which monitors the service level of your providers, helping you make sure the service lives up to what you were promised.

Considering all this, there are cost savings and operational benefit that Service providers like BLOKWORX can bring to this piece of your business. You should always look to providers who specialize in WAN and multi-site location management. If you choose well, you will receive greater service at a lower cost – and most importantly, peace of mind.

About Robert

Robert Boles is the Co-Founder and President of BLOKWORX. Robert brings more than 14 years of solving real business challenges for clients – ranging from individual and family-owned businesses to Fortune 500 corporations. Robert's core belief in Security, Reliability, and delivering a Positive User experience drives BLOKWORX's fundamental practice of building scalable, secure, IT Solutions that users enjoy working with.

Prior to founding BLOKWORX, Robert was an Enterprise Systems Engineer for an international communications company providing Advanced IP services based on Cisco, Juniper, HP, and Checkpoint, among others. Robert was a highly-specialized engineer, one of only four in a company of over 200,000 employees. Robert worked cooperatively with Product Marketing, Sales Organizations, and Operations to create a suite of managed service offerings, and defined many of the processes and technology selected within the projects. Then, as a Systems Engineer directly supporting the sales organizations, Robert designed, successfully implemented, and seamlessly transitioned to the support team over 100 managed network solutions for clients among over 1,400 global locations. As a subject matter expert, Robert educated clients, engineering, and sales teams on the Advanced IP product portfolio, which consisted of Wide Area Network Services, Network Security Services, Colocation and Advanced Hosting.

After seven years with the company, Robert made the decision to go back to his roots, and create an IT service provider which met his vision. BLOKWORX was driven from the start to provide fuller, friendlier, more complete IT Solutions for its clients. Given BLOKWORX's exceptional client retention and long-term relationships, the formula is working.

Robert was raised in Arbuckle, CA, a rural, agricultural town outside Sacramento. His father was a local businessman, and his mother managed the local bank. Following high school, Robert joined the United States Marine Corps and served in Operation Desert Shield/Desert Storm. This early-life experience impressed upon Robert the value of relationships, doing right by people, and teamwork. These were lessons which, in application, have fueled the BLOKWORX philosophy that, "If we always take care of our clients by doing right by them in the most honest way, and have fun in the process, then everything else will take care of itself."

A featured speaker for both internal and client presentations and events, Robert is widely valued for his integrity, passion for technology, and ability to solve business challenges. Robert lives in San Francisco, CA with his wife Sarah, son Jack, and dog Chewie.

BLOKWORX is a member of the National Veteran Owned Business Association (NaVOBA), and proudly supports CompTia Troops to Tech.

More information available at:
www.blokworx.com
www.troopstotechcareers.org
Email: Robert@blokworx.com
Office: 415-571-4300 x826

CHAPTER 21

EMAIL

BY SCOTT SPIRO

Without question, email has become a staple for businesses around the world and we have become dependent upon it as a mainstay in our interaction with one another. There are definite benefits to this electronic marvel that enables people from different continents to share not only brief messages but also documents containing volumes of pages in mere seconds. How did the world function without this great invention and where would we be today if we didn't have the opportunity to be clutched by its intrigue on a daily basis? There are other electronic mediums that try to compete, but email continues to be one of the most versatile tools in the businessperson's arsenal.

While email has become one of the fundamental tools for business functionality, much like other variations of virtual communication, it also has an addictive nature to it. For some it becomes a distraction because they feel obligated to read every message the minute it comes through. Many will check their email as soon as their eyes open in the morning and before they slither from the comfort of their bed. In the 90's it had become such a craze that a movie was made based on the three infamous words that we all wanted to hear in that decade, "You've got mail."

Email has evolved over the years to be both good and bad. The accomplishments made possible by email have propelled us to more efficiency and productivity. On the other hand, spammers and unscrupulous individuals have used it to gain access to information that doesn't belong to them and to cause untold headaches for the victims that have fallen prey to their destructive ploys. This chapter is focused on helping you to capitalize on the benefits of email as well as aid you in taking steps to protect yourself and your business from the ravages of the unethical by putting in place the proper safeguards.

DECIDING WHERE TO HOUSE YOUR EMAIL

For many new companies just getting started, both large and small, it may not make sense to house email servers on-site. Interestingly enough, cloud-based email was usually leveraged by smaller firms with 10 employees or less. However, as prices have come down and cloud technologies have become more accepted, even larger firms with hundreds of employees have chosen cloud options.

From a technical standpoint, it takes a tremendous amount of resources to keep local email systems up and running. Ultimately, it could possibly cost the business more money to pay for the upkeep and support to keep those servers running 24/7. By putting those systems in the cloud you basically remove the local support that is required and you're able to have better redundancy and security in the process.

If you choose to work with an email provider, the big question you must consider is related to support. What kind of support will you receive from your email vendor? Many of the large companies that supply this service aren't necessarily known for the quality of their support. When you have an emergency situation how long will it take for you to get a hold of someone who actually knows what they're talking about? You have to be concerned about that because when your email is not working, your business is basically at a standstill.

Working with a reputable and qualified professional Information Technology (IT) provider can be advantageous because they have a tremendous amount of experience working with a number of email providers and can recommend one to you. Also, they usually have a direct line to the email vendor support personnel. So, if you have a problem with your email, you can call your IT provider directly and they will usually be able to help you get your problem resolved promptly. They have built these relationships over the years through various industry connections and you can be sure they will reach out to the right resources on your behalf.

Finally, if you choose to house your email server onsite, keep in mind that in addition to supporting the server, you will have to actually buy the software. When you put your email service in the cloud you are basically paying someone else to manage the system and you will not have to buy the software. You are in essence "renting" the email system from them and there are very small upfront costs by setting it up that way. You also have the benefit of having that system outside the office. So, if your power goes off or your Internet goes out you will be able to continue to communicate via your mobile phone or from another location because you will be leveraging your vendor's network.

EMAIL SECURITY

One of the primary ways that malware, spam, viruses and worms can get into your network is through email. There are other ways they can come in as well, but email is definitely one of the easiest ways to infiltrate your network. The use of email in this destructive fashion is called *phishing*. Basically, this is the process unscrupulous people use to go "fishing" for your information. The strategy is typically designed in such a way as to fool you into thinking you are interacting with one of your family members, friends, acquaintances or business associates. It may even look like the email is being sent from a reputable company. The email is designed to get you to give them information such as your social security number, credit card number, or user name and password. If one of your employees clicks on one of these emails and gives any of the requested information it basically then bypasses all the security you have on your network. You can have all the firewalls and protection measures set up, but as soon as you click on one of the available options you have opened the door to a damaging infiltration to your network and it immediately starts to go to work collecting data.

Any business must take email security very seriously and there are a few things they need to have in place for protection. It is imperative to have a good piece of spam protection software that is on the mail server if it is an in-house server or the company with whom the business contracts – must have a high-quality spam protection in place. If you use a vendor for your email, you will want to make sure the spam protection provided by that vendor meets your business needs. If necessary, there are additional third party products that will give you more protection capability.

Email must be protected when it is coming in as well as when it's going out. If you contract a virus as a result of phishing, you want to make sure your spam filter doesn't allow that same virus to be spread by an email you send out to an unsuspecting recipient. It can be a very embarrassing moment if it is discovered that your business is the source for spam or virus proliferation. Additionally, your email server could get "black listed." If that happens you won't be able to send out any email at all. A spam filter will basically "scrub" the email before it goes out to make sure it doesn't contain any spam or viruses that would corrupt someone else's network.

One of the features that some email vendors allow is called "Protective Email Addresses" or "Email on the Fly." This will protect your email address from getting spammed by setting up a slightly different email addresses for different uses. For example, if you buy things from eBay, you could set up a specific email for eBay so that if someone was able to get a hold of that address and start spamming you, you could simply turn that email address off.

You can also leverage additional email filtering, enabling you to screen messages from senders that are not on a recipient's allow list. For example, you may want to block mail from certain countries. There is a wide array of parameters you can establish to filter the emails that try to reach you.

Additionally, you can use a white listing and black listing technique. You can white list specific domains, which will allow those particular domains to be sent to you. Whereas there may be other domains you will want to blacklist so they cannot reach you. For example, there are a lot of viruses to watch for from China and Eastern Europe. Your business should be using a product that allows you to block countries, designated users and specific domains. Your spam filter should automatically blacklist anything that comes through that meets the blacklist criteria that has been established.

When you use an outside vendor for your email, their spam protection may not be enough for your business needs. If that is the case, you will want to have a third party spam filter in place. Your IT provider will be able to assist you in the selection of the spam filter that best fits your needs.

In addition to the spam and malware protection that is on your email server or provided by your email vendor, the virus protection that runs on your local computer will also have the capability to scan the email. This is just another layer of protection you can employ.

EMAIL ARCHIVING

For some companies that have compliance regulations by which they must abide, they need to be able to keep their email indefinitely or for a specified period of time. There are several companies that provide archiving technology that meet specific compliance regulations. Companies with those types of archiving needs will be served well by these archiving specialists.

EMAIL ENCRYPTION

Encryption is utilized when you send an email and you want to make sure your recipient is the one opening your email and that no one else is able to read the email during the transfer process. The email can be encrypted, sent to the recipient, and then the recipient can decrypt the email using a password. There are companies that specialize in encryption. It can be useful to engage a service that will encrypt an email automatically based on specific key words or other established criteria. Encryptions services are typically used by businesses that have regulatory compliance standards to which they must adhere, such as the healthcare industry.

CREATE AN ACCEPTABLE USE POLICY

Businesses should have an IT Acceptable Use Policy in place which informs their employees what the employer deems acceptable use of business email resources. This policy also specifies to the employee that their business email belongs to the employer, not the employee. This document should be signed by each employee so there is documentation that each employee understands and agrees to abide by the established policy. This policy should be part of the company's new employee orientation process and can be part of the employee handbook.

In addition to the policy, the company should implement an email monitoring strategy for specific key words and for specific file types. If you are in healthcare, for example, HIPAA requires you to monitor email transmissions to make sure protected health information is not being distributed inappropriately. Additional monitoring criteria a business may want to institute include social security numbers and any inappropriate material.

EMAIL EDUCATION

If someone is not educated about email usage it is possible they could be fooled by a phishing email and could place your business in jeopardy. You should offer an education opportunity to employees annually or semi-annually to make sure they are aware of the latest threats that have been discovered that can possibly infiltrate the company network through email. This training should educate them on what they should be watching for and how they should report any suspicious emails. Some clues that an email could possibly be spam include spelling errors; grammatical errors; request for a social security number, bank account number or credit card number; and request for a password. Sometimes an email will ask you to click on something. When this happens, it is always best to right click on the link, then copy the link and paste it into a browser to see where the link is connected. A lot of times it will be a foreign website with a Russian or Chinese suffix at the end. These items will also be beneficial to include in a training class.

EMAIL ETIQUETTE

When communicating by email, pay attention to the sender's writing style. Some people will write very short emails, maybe just a few words or only a couple of sentences. I have found that if you can mimic their writing style you can get better results because their writing style is an indication of how they prefer to communicate.

In my emails I will often use bullet points and numbers. I try to utilize those to offer a very concise and precise message. When I have finished writing my email I look it over to determine how I can make it more precise and how I can use fewer words. Today people are so busy they don't want to take the time to read through paragraphs of content. If you want your email to be read, keep it short and concise. If your email is too long, the recipient may skip over it with the intention of reading it later when they have more time. That increases the possibility that the email will be forgotten.

There are also services available that help keep your email organized. There is a service called SaneBox that is very helpful for email management. There are also different helpful methodologies, such as the Getting Things Done® (GTD®) method promoted by David Allen. I personally get over 200 emails a day and most people in business have similar amounts of email they receive on a daily basis. It is very easy to get bogged down and distracted by email while other things that need your attention are waiting. Checking your email only at specific times during the day may help keep you from constantly being distracted by email throughout the day.

ASK FOR HELP

As you know, email can be both a curse and a blessing. It all depends on how you use it and how you protect it. I encourage you to seek out a qualified IT provider to assist you with the establishment of your email account or to help you with any email issues that arise. Sometimes going it alone can create more problems than it solves. A trusted IT professional can save you time and effort while giving you solutions that will make you more efficient and profitable.

About Scott

Scott Spiro is founder and President of Computer Solutions Group, Inc (CSG), and author of the book Hassle Free Computer Support. In 2013, CSG was named one of the top 100 I.T. firms in the nation by tradesite MSPmentor.com.

In addition to solving the typical I.T. challenges most businesses face, Scott has focused his own efforts in helping his clients and their families battle Cybercrime, Cyberbullying, and other harmful technologies. A member of the U.S. Secret Service Electronic Crimes Task Force, Scott is dedicated to protecting both businesses and consumers from the potential dangers of being "connected" 24/7 to their computers. Additionally, with two small children of his own and some recent health issues, Scott began development of new programs designed to help business owners better manage their technology and lifestyle. This sometimes means turning it all off in order to focus on not just their businesses, but also their health and loved ones.

A graduate of UCLA, Scott had originally planned to go into the Entertainment field. However, a knack for technology and an interest in entrepreneurship led him along a different path. Scott has been featured by the N.Y. Times, KTLA Channel 5 News, KFWB, and was nominated by the Century City Chamber of Commerce for their *Men of Achievement* award. Scott enjoys participation in the LA5 Rotary Club, EO, and any activities that involve spending time with his family and friends.

CHAPTER 22

EMPLOYEE MONITORING

BY SEAN ROBERTSON

When the discussion of monitoring or limiting the computer-related activity of employees comes up with my clients, it's not unusual for them to say things to me like, "My employees are good people."… "No need for 'secret squirrel' here."… and, "My employees are my friends and they would never hurt me." I've heard these statements hundreds of times from small business owners and it can sometimes be a difficult conversation. The unfortunate thing is that some employers don't heed my advice to put proper monitoring measures in place until I get that "second" call to discuss the cleanup and aftermath of an employee (or partner) problem that caused a significant issue.

Recently, I worked with a small multi-national company with three offices in three countries with approximately 35 office employees collectively. This company was growing fast and was using acquisition as a means to fuel their growth. After one acquisition, they hired the previous business owner to be the General Manager of the US-based operation.

The integration went very smoothly from an operations perspective, but there were a few challenges that almost lead to the bankruptcy of this business. In the excitement of the new acquisition, no one looked at the technology being used by the acquired company other than the accounting system.

One Friday afternoon, which often seems to be the day problems are discovered, one of my senior technicians received a phone call from the client. The phone call started with, "I'm so glad you're available. We haven't been able to access any of our data for three days. I've got to get payroll done and I've got to invoice my clients. Can you help?"

After a small bit of investigating, the problem was becoming more defined. Whenever a file was opened, it couldn't be read. Microsoft Office and every other piece of software said the files were not readable. The files could be seen, they weren't gone, but they just couldn't be opened. Two of my senior technicians spent the next 72 hours trying desperately to understand what was wrong.

The hardware passed all of our diagnostics, but we still couldn't open the documents. The data showed no signs of corruption, but couldn't be read. At first, this was happening on just one server, and then it spread. At the end of the third day of attempted recovery, the data on the second server now had the same problem. And, because of the way the client elected to perform backups, the backup data had the same problem. At this point, there was only one known useable copy of this client's data and it was seven months old.

Not having this data would lead to significant financial issues as well as service delivery issues for this business. An additional concern in this situation was that the client was also storing someone else's data 'as a favor' and that data was also not usable.

Overnight on Monday, almost every computer in the office was scanned for virus and malware. Unfortunately, every computer came back positive with various forms of malware. However, none of the malware seemed to be related to the problem. There was, however, one computer that we were unable to scan that night because it was not made available to us. It was the computer used by the former owner and now General Manager. He had "forgotten" to give us access.

He had also "forgotten" to tell us that on the previous Monday, his computer had become infected with Cryptolocker, a nasty piece of malware which holds your data ransom. It does this by encrypting any and all data it can find and then demands a payment to have it decrypted. In fact, one version of this doesn't even make the demand, it simply waits for users to search the Internet for a solution and then sells decryption software through a legitimate-looking website.

There is of course more to the story. It was discovered that the General Manager had picked up the virus while surfing inappropriate sites while at work. After realizing he was responsible for allowing the entrance of a virus, he was embarrassed and spent a day trying to solve the problem himself. He then called in a local technician to solve the problem. The local technician wasn't very experienced and removed the virus without informing anyone of potential consequences.

All of this could have been prevented if the proper monitoring protocols were in place. If for some reason the website was not blocked, the monitoring system's antivirus system would have stopped the delivery of the virus. The crisis would have been averted and money would have been saved.

The client eventually spent over $35,000 and fifteen days of downtime, but we were not able to recover all of their data. Instead we had to use a backup from their most recent server upgrade that was seven months old. Fortunately, this company had the resources to recover their data. However, not every company is so fortunate, and the consequences of losing every piece of data you have can be dire – to say the least.

There are many things that the company involved in this story could have and should have done differently. Backups weren't performed properly, desktop and gateway antivirus wasn't in place, and all users had "super user" access. These are all very significant problems. But the crux of this particular problem stemmed from the fact that there was no employee monitoring system in place.

When most people think employee monitoring, they think about stopping employees from visiting non-work related sites. This is of course with good reason. Recent surveys indicate that 39% of employees spend between 1 and 10 hours per week surfing non-work related web sites.

However, there is another significant risk of not having an employee monitoring system. It's a legal and a financial risk. If you permit (or do not stop) employees from visiting objectionable websites, you are placing your company in a place of vulnerability in many ways. Imagine an employee viewing pornographic material on their work computer. Now picture another employee walking up behind that employee and seeing the pornographic material on the screen. You are now potentially on the hook for a harassment lawsuit or some other type of litigation.

Related to this topic, we were called to a business to investigate a problem of a very slow network. As we were telling the employees what we were going to investigate, one person appeared very, very concerned and asked about their right to privacy. Through our investigation, we found that not only was that employee keeping child pornography on his company-issued notebook, he was distributing it to other people on the Internet through the corporate network. In this particular case, the authorities seized that employee's company-issued notebook and another company computer and kept them for six months. Unfortunately, the business was not able to gain access to any of the company-related files on those devices because it became evidence in a police investigation. Think of the ramifications of this incident. The company lost a computer and notebook, experienced work disruption because of the investigation and had to pay for IT services to discover a problem. Add to this the potential negative press a situation like this can bring to the company, even though it was an employee of the company and not the company itself being targeted in the investigation.

Recovering employee time and preventing lawsuits is obviously appealing and the savings can be significant. But really, those savings pale in comparison to the cost of losing your business. Both of the examples above could have been avoided with an employee monitoring system.

Many times we've gone into companies to do an audit and have found 10 or 15 people who are no longer employees but still have access to the network and have recent logins recorded. This happens all the time. While I consider this to be the utmost negligence in IT security, it's not a rare incident.

Small businesses are preyed upon by the bad guys because the small business owner typically has limited resources to protect their data. People assume that bad guys are stupid, but they're not. You can actually hire crime as a service today. You can go to an underground bazaar and subscribe to almost anything you want. You can hire a hit man, buy drugs, or buy a block of credit card numbers. The selection of crime activity is almost limitless. This is not an exaggeration that is espoused by the Information Technology community to sell their services. There is a very real threat that exists to individuals as well as to business interests. Unfortunately, many times individuals and businesses don't fully understand this risk until tragedy strikes them.

As a business owner or leader, it is your responsibility to take a proactive approach to put into place monitoring resources that will protect your business concerns and your employees while they are conducting work on your behalf. Below are some suggested steps you can take to protect your business and improve employee productivity:

1. CREATE AN ACCEPTABLE USE POLICY

This policy should be in writing and should define what employees are allowed and not allowed to do with company resources such as smart phones, computers, tablets and Internet access while in the office or out of the office. A qualified IT provider can help you develop your policy. But, here are some things to consider as you develop this policy:

- What type of web sites are employees allowed to visit?
- Can they download movies or music?
- Are they allowed to have non-work material on their computers?
- Are their children allowed to surf the web or watch movies on the device?
- Are they allowed to install software on their own or do they require permission?
- What is being monitored and why?
- What can the employee expect for privacy?
- Will you monitor email?
- How will you monitor non-work email addresses they access via company assets?
- Tell them they must not do anything illegal using any work-related devices or equipment.

2. BE UPFRONT WITH YOUR EMPLOYEES

There is no reason to hide the fact that you monitor and control employee use of company resources. Make sure your Acceptable Use Policy is in writing and that every employee has a copy. It may be a good idea to include your Acceptable Use Policy in your Employee Handbook. Your policy should be discussed with existing employees and should be part of your new employee orientation. Choose the method of communication that works best for you, but be sure to let them know you are monitoring, why you are monitoring and what you are monitoring.

Often small business owners don't want their employees to feel like "Big Brother" is watching over them. However, that sometimes leads to financial loss. It is best to monitor and prevent a problem rather than clean up the chaos caused by a problem. Tell people what you are doing, how you are doing it, and how you will use the information you collect. Let them know that you are not necessarily monitoring any one person specifically, although you can and sometimes may have to monitor specific individuals if there are reasonable suspicions. But, more importantly, let them know that you are looking for patterns to protect the business. You will find that most people will readily adapt to your established policies and accept it as a condition of employment.

3. START FILTERING AND MONITORING

Your main goal is to protect your business from what employees intentionally or unintentionally may do to harm your company. At the perimeter you can set up a Unified Threat Management (UTM) system that looks at all the information that comes into and goes out of the network. UTM can monitor and dictate what websites can be looked at by employees and blocks viruses and other malicious software before it gets to your network. You want to protect your business from sites that can potentially bring harm to your internal systems. This will prevent employees from accessing sites that may be full of malware or are inappropriate as determined by your corporate protocol. This is the first level of monitoring that I recommend businesses employ.

You will also want to make sure you filter all outbound and inbound emails. Company secrets can disappear via outbound email and spam and viruses can be introduced via incoming email. If an employee inadvertently becomes a spammer, your filter will catch it and protect your company's Internet reputation.

The next step would be to look at desktop and laptop monitoring and filtering. You will need to decide if you are trying to protect, monitor or both. If needed, you can conduct specific device monitoring to determine what applications a particular employee had open, when they were opened and whether or not that employee was actually working. Specific device monitoring can record every keystroke made by the employee if that becomes necessary.

When you have mobile devices that leave the safety of the inter-office network the mobile devices can be misused and can become vulnerable to acquiring a malicious virus. However, device monitoring can mitigate that risk by applying the same filters on any mobile device. Basically, the same controls that are in place for your network can also be placed on all your mobile devices. It's a little tougher to monitor smart phones as there are very few tools to help manage those devices. There are some, but they aren't very robust.

Filtering and monitoring not only keeps the bad guys from getting in, but it also keeps protected information from getting out. You can put filters on network and mobile devices that say, for example, "Make sure that nothing containing a social security number ever gets sent. If it is included in an email, forward a copy of the email to this monitoring station because it violates our established terms of usage." While you can't look for specific documents, you can look for key words or key indicators that indicate something wrong may be happening.

If you are concerned about the protection of your Intellectual Property or trade secrets, there is software that can be installed that will prevent the unauthorized usage of any USB drives in your computers. If USB drives are used, they must be a USB drive that is issued by the company with a certain identification number and specific encryption. When it is plugged in, the computer will recognize it as an authorized USB and will allow information to be transferred from the device to the USB or from the USB to the device. This is not as much a monitoring activity as it is a prevention activity, but it is a methodology that can certainly save a business under certain circumstances.

4. REVIEW AND UTILIZE THE REPORTS

There will be numerous reports you will want to monitor because they have the ability to save you a lot of time, money and overall headaches. Essentially you want to look at the type of traffic coming into your network and going out from your network to see if it makes sense. It's not usually about finding out that a specific employee has done something wrong, although it could certainly lead to that, but it's about being alerted to potential problems because of idiosyncrasies in the data.

When monitoring reports, you will want to be looking for the exceptions and things outside your normal activity. For example, let's say you had 7,000 visits to sites that are trying to download malware to your network. You may recognize that as unusual because you usually get just one or two a week. That tells you there is a problem. Increased attempts to reach a site that has malware on it probably means one of your machines is infected with something and it's trying to spread or call home for instructions.

Your email reports will also give you important information. For example, if your company normally sends around 1,000 emails per week and this week you see there were 50,000 outbound emails; that may be indicative of a problem. Increased mail activity may be an indication that there is a spammer trying to send email through your network.

Make sure you are using the report data appropriately and efficiently. If there is an indication of a problem, have the problem researched further and resolve the issue before it becomes an even greater problem. If your investigation leads you to a specific employee, be committed to appropriately discuss with the employee questionable behavior or activity. There is little point in identifying a problem if you are not committed to resolving the problem to protect your business.

5. TAKE A PROACTIVE APPROACH TO EMPLOYEE MONITORING

If you have a business, you **MUST** put monitoring safeguards in place. If you don't, it is an indication of the value or lack of value you place on your work. Sometimes business owners will use cost as a reason to not have appropriate monitoring in place. It may surprise you to know that monitoring can be done at a very reasonable price. In fact, the price of not monitoring is too high to not have the proper monitoring practices in place.

About Sean

Sean Robertson has been working with business technology for more than thirty years. When he was only sixteen years old, while still attending high school, he co-founded Universal Programming in Halifax, Nova Scotia. After working his way through school developing payroll and manufacturing systems, he accepted his first "real job" supporting and installing accounting, point of sale and front desk systems throughout Atlantic Canada. After settling in Moncton, New Brunswick, Sean accepted a leadership role with General Electric Appliances Canada and was able to further round out his experience by accepting leadership roles in Technology, Customer Service, Logistics and becoming certified as a Six Sigma Green Belt.

After several years with GE, Sean accepted a role with an international manufacturing company leading the Customer Service, Manufacturing Operations and Technology teams as Vice President Operations and Chief Information Officer.

In 2007, Sean recognized an opportunity to bring enterprise level technology management to small and medium business and founded Strategic Technology Associates (STAI).

Spending so many years leading customer service and technology teams at an Executive level provided a strong foundation for building a client-focused, results-oriented information technology services company. Sean is often heard saying how proud he is that his first customer is still a valued customer.

Strategic Technology Associates operates throughout Atlantic Canada, using a different strategy than most other technology service providers. The business model used by STAI doesn't permit profit from client computer problems. Instead; networks, desktops and servers are managed proactively to minimize downtime and save money for clients.

You can find Sean at:
sean@stai.ca
www.twitter.com/StrategicTech
www.facebook.com/getstrategic

CPSIA information can be obtained at www.ICGtesting.com
Printed in the USA
LVOW10*2337210514

386834LV00007B/35/P